Early Childhood Reading Activities

Literacy, Language, & Learning

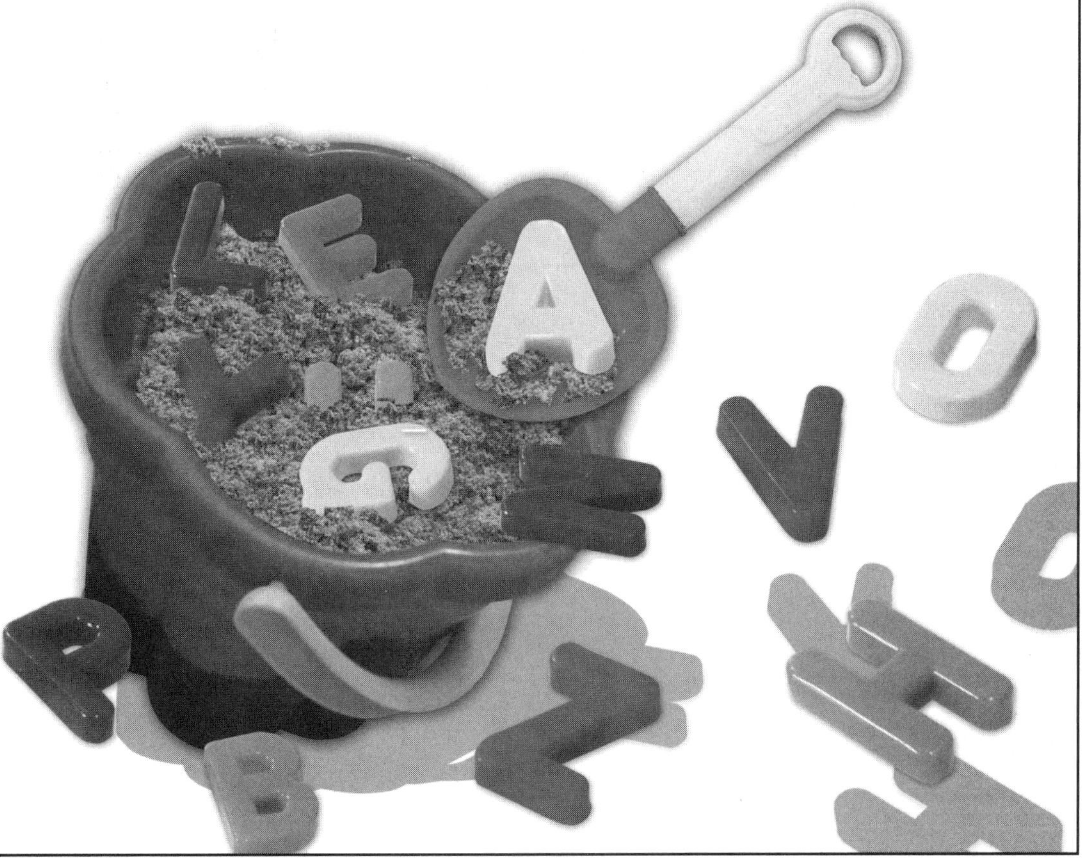

Author
Denise LaRose, M.A.Ed

Credits

Publishing Credits

Dona Herweck Rice, *Editor-in-Chief*; Lee Aucoin, *Creative Director*; Don Tran, *Print Production Manager;* Timothy J. Bradley, *Illustration Manager*; Jodene Smith, M.A., *Editor;* Leslie Huber, M.A., *Assistant Editor;* Lee Aucoin, *Cover Designer;* Robin Erickson, *Interior Layout Designer;* Corinne Burton, M.S. Ed., *Publisher*

Standards Compendium, Copyright 2004 McREL

Shell Education
5301 Oceanus Drive
Huntington Beach, CA 92649-1030
http://www.shelleducation.com
ISBN 978-0-7439-0698-9
© 2010 Shell Educational Publishing, Inc.

The classroom teacher may reproduce copies of materials in this book for classroom use only. The reproduction of any part for an entire school or school system is strictly prohibited. No part of this publication may be transmitted, stored, or recorded in any form without written permission from the publisher.

Table of Contents

Introduction
Introduction and Research 4
How to Use this Book 5
Observing Students for Assessment 7
Standards Correlations 8
Standards Correlation Chart 9

Identifying Letters
Ball Toss 10
Cookie Letters 12
Doggie, Doggie 16
Letter Walk 20
Rock Wall 22
Letter Scoop 24
Smart Drivers 26
I'm Going on a Trip 32

Letter-Sound Associations
Dinnertime 34
Free the Animals 38
Letter Detective 44
Name Game 46
Night Sky Match 48
What Am I? 60
Letter Shake 66
Blend Detective 70

Reading Sight Words
Witches' Brew 76
Bowling for Sight Words 78

Reading Sight Words (cont.)
Word-O 80
Find Your Partner 88
Fish for Supper 90
Sight Word Search 92
Pasta Bowl 94
Hopscotch 96
Musical Chairs 98
Off to School We Go! 106
Penny Words 114
Pin the Word on the Donkey ... 116
Go Fish 120

Forming Sentences
Beat the Clock 122
Question Game 124
Follow the Rainbow 130
It's Raining 134
Puzzle Words 142
Word Roundup 148

Appendix A
References Cited 154

Appendix B
Uppercase Alphabet Cards 155

Appendix C
Lowercase Alphabet Cards 162

Appendix D
Sight Word Cards 169

Introduction and Research

Today, more than ever, greater demands are being placed on the classroom teacher to instruct children how to read. Educators are guided by national, state, and local mandates to ensure that students become successful readers. These mandates apply to all students, including young learners as they enter preschool and kindergarten. The key to teaching these emergent readers is to provide a balanced program that is developmentally appropriate. *Early Childhood Reading Activities* is a resource that can be useful to you as a classroom teacher as you guide students in meeting these mandates.

The activities and games throughout this book focus on letter identification, letter-sound associations, sight words, and forming sentences. Letter identification involves being able to state the names of letters when they are shown at random. Research shows that the letter-identification knowledge a kindergarten student has is a very good predictor of future reading success (Burns, Griffin, and Snow 1998; Robinson, 1991; Wylie, 1969). Equally important is the connection the student is able to make between **letters and sounds**. We know that reading is a meaning-making adventure, but if a child cannot decode words, then meaning is lost. Being able to make the connection between **letters and sounds** is critical (Dakin, 1999; Dwyer & Ralston, 1999). **Sight words** are also an important aspect of literacy. Children need a core group of sight words that they can easily and quickly read without having to decode. These words are often viewed as anchor words. These words give children the encouragement that they can read a passage because they see so many words they know by sight. As children are able to recognize many sight words quickly, reading becomes more fluent (Ehri, 2005; Monroe and Staunton, 2000). Reading sight words out of context is not the goal, but having the ability to read these words in **sentences** helps a student get one step closer to becoming a true reader. A true reader is one who pulls many strategies together in order to read and understand the text. *Early Childhood Reading Activities* will help students develop some of these critical strategies.

What better way is there to learn than by having fun? Children can achieve success by learning in an environment that is enjoyable and considered a fun place to be (Buehler, 1992). Researchers believe that playful activities that focus on the sound structure of language support and promote literacy development (Yopp and Yopp, 2000; Burns, Griffin, and Snow 1999). **The activities and games in this book are appealing to young learners because they are fun**. Since they are so inviting, children focus on the concepts and in turn grasp literacy concepts more quickly. Younger, active children need to be involved in fun activities and games that address their developmental needs. Teachers need to teach children how to read. By using this resource, both goals can be met.

The activities and games in this book are geared toward small and large groups. If you are playing a small-group game, remember to utilize parent volunteers. Parents are an important aspect in the education of their children. Research has shown that the more involved a parent is with his or her child's education, the more successful that child will be (Shaver and Walls, 1998; Carter 2002). What better way for a parent to be involved than to actually help out in the classroom!

This book will complement any reading program you are currently using. The goal is for children to learn to read while having fun. Your students will enjoy the games and learn to love reading!

How to Use This Book

Selecting Activities and Games

The activities and games in this book are divided into four sections: **Identifying Letters**, **Letter and Sound Associations**, **Sight Words**, and **Forming Sentences**. See the table of contents for specific page numbers on which each section begins. Begin by reviewing the activities and games according to the skill you want; however, do not be limited by the sections. Many of the activities and games in this book can be adapted to any of the skills listed. For example, the activity "Cookie Letters" is in the Identifying Letters section of the book; however, the activity can easily be adapted to have students practice sight words. Some suggestions for adaptations are provided at the bottom of each teacher-direction page.

Preparation and Storage

The materials needed for each activity or game are listed on the teacher-direction pages. Specific patterns or game boards that may be needed are on the pages following the teacher directions. The patterns can be photocopied in black and white from this book and then colored by hand, or they can be **printed in full color from the interactive whiteboard-compatible teacher resource CD**. Glue the pieces to construction paper or thin cardboard to create more durable pieces. Consider laminating all the pieces for durability, too. Enlarging the patterns and game boards is another option you may wish to consider. This is especially helpful for the game boards. Use a copy machine with an enlarge option or copy the pattern onto a transparency. Place the transparency on an overhead projector and trace the image onto a piece of poster board.

A 9" x 12" (23 cm x 30 cm) manila envelope with a clasp works well to store most of the pieces needed for each game. You may want to create an envelope for each game in order to keep the pieces organized and easy to access. Be sure to clearly label each envelope with the name of the game. Once the materials needed to play the game are gathered and the game pieces created, preparation for the activities and games is minimal. Consider photocopying the teacher-direction page and cutting out the "Activity Procedures." Glue these to the front of the manila envelope. These directions tell how to do the activity or to play the game. The envelope can be handed to a parent volunteer or classroom aide. Minimal verbal directions will be needed because everything is contained within the envelope.

How to Use This Book (cont.)

Introducing the Activities and Games

Even though many of the games are designed for a small group, you may wish to introduce the activities and games in a whole-class setting. You may have to select a few students to help you demonstrate how to do the activity or play the game, or you may be able to modify the activity slightly in order to accommodate the whole class. An overhead projector, document camera, or interactive whiteboard are other methods of introducing an activity or game to the whole class. Photocopy necessary patterns onto transparencies, which can then be projected on a screen for the whole class to see. Finally, the activities and games can be introduced in a small group. Be sure to consistently describe and play the game with each group to which you introduce it. When the children play the game independent of teacher supervision, you will want them all to play by the same rules. Consider your class and the particular activity to decide the best method of introduction for your students.

It is useful to remind students each time an activity or game is introduced or played that the purpose is to practice reading, not to see who can win. Everyone wins if letters, sounds, and sight words are learned and practiced in a fun way. You may wish to make it a policy that everyone gets a sticker, kudos from the teacher, or other small prizes if they participate in the activity or game. This reinforces the fact that everyone is a winner when he or she practices reading.

Parent Volunteers and Classroom Aides

Utilize parent volunteers and classroom aides to assist you in preparing the materials in this book. Often, parents who are unable to volunteer in the classroom are willing to assist in coloring or assembling materials that are sent home. Be sure to provide directions and all of the materials necessary for the volunteers to complete the task. Providing a "return by [date]" slip also helps you get the materials back in a timely manner.

Parent volunteers, classroom aides, and cross-age tutors are excellent resources for monitoring small groups as they play games. Provide game monitors with directions on how the activity is to be done or how the games are to be played. Remind the monitors that the purpose of the activity or game is to practice reading.

Who Goes First?

Who goes first? This is probably one of the most hotly contested questions when children play games. You will want to have this question answered prior to introducing an activity or game to the students. You may wish to have a set procedure for all the activities and games that can be used for determining who goes first, or you may wish to select a different procedure for each activity and game. Either way, having the procedure established will eliminate many arguments. Some suggestions for determining who goes first are listed below.

- Roll a die.
- Draw straws.
- Pull numbers out of a hat or other container.
- Flip a coin.
- Play rock, paper, scissors.
- Choose the person wearing the most items of clothing of a selected color.
- Select the youngest/oldest.
- Have ladies/gentlemen go first.
- Have students play in alphabetical or reverse alphabetical order.

Observing Students for Assessment

Take advantage of the great opportunity to assess students as you observe them participating in the activities or playing the games. There are a variety of assessment tools, such as checklists, anecdotal notes, and data-capture sheets that can be used for documenting observations. Data-capture sheets are especially helpful to document events, behaviors, and skills that can be used to provide an overall picture of what a student is capable of and areas in which the student still needs to develop. Data-capture sheets usually incorporate a checklist of specific behaviors to be observed and space for observation notes. Below is a general form that can be used as you observe students participating in reading activities and games. The first two observations are general observations that can be applied to almost any activity or game. Fill in the bottom two observations to include specific skills to observe, such as "Matches uppercase and lowercase letters."

Y = Yes, behavior exhibited   S = behavior somewhat exhibited   N = behavior not exhibited

Student Name _____ Date_____

	Y	S	N	
1.	☐	☐	☐	Exhibited an adequate understanding of the activity/game.
2.	☐	☐	☐	Displayed knowledge of vocabulary related to the activity/game.
3.	☐	☐	☐	_____
4.	☐	☐	☐	_____

Overall, the student's performance [circle choice] expectations...

went beyond   met overall   met partial   met minimal   did not meet

Notes:

Standards Correlations

Standards Correlations

Shell Education is committed to producing educational materials that are research and standards based. In this effort, we have correlated all of our products to the academic standards of all 50 states, the District of Columbia, and the Department of Defense Dependent Schools.

How to Find Standards Correlations

To print a customized correlation report of this product for your state, visit our website at **http://www.sheddeducation.com** and follow the on-screen directions. If you require assistance in printing correlation reports, please contact Customer Service at 1-877-777-3450.

Purpose and Intent of Standards

The No Child Left Behind legislation mandates that all states adopt academic standards that identify the skills students will learn in kindergarten through grade twelve. While many states had already adopted academic standards prior to NCLB, the legislation set requirements to ensure the standards were detailed and comprehensive.

Standards are designed to focus instruction and guide adoption of curricula. Standards are statements that describe the criteria necessary for students to meet specific academic goals. They define the knowledge, skills, and content students should acquire at each level. Standards are also used to develop standardized tests to evaluate students' academic progress.

Teachers are required to demonstrate how their lessons meet state standards. State standards are used in development of all of our products, so educators can be assured they meet the academic requirements of each state.

McREL Compendium

We use the Mid-continent Research for Education and Learning (McREL) Compendium to create standards correlations. Each year, McREL analyzes state standards and revises the compendium. By following this procedure, McREL is able to produce a general compilation of national standards. Each lesson in this product is based on one or more McREL standards. The chart on the following page lists each standard taught in this product and the page numbers for the corresponding lessons.

Standards Correlation Chart

Standard 5

Uses the general skills and strategies of the reading process

Benchmark	Lesson and Page Number
Standard 5.6 **Level: Pre-K** Knows some letters of the alphabet, such as those in the student's own name	Ball Toss .... 10–11 Cookie Letters .... 12–15 Doggie, Doggie .... 16–19 Letter Walk .... 20–21 Rock Wall .... 22–23 Letter Scoop .... 24–25 Smart Drivers .... 26–31 I'm Going on a Trip 32–33
Standard 5.3 **Level 1: K–2** Uses basic elements of phonetical analysis (e.g., common letter-sound relationships, beginning and ending consonants, vowel sounds, blends, word patterns) to decode unknown words	Dinnertime .... 34–37 Free the Animals .... 38–43 Letter Detective .... 44–45 Name Game .... 46–47 Night Sky Match .... 48–59 What Am I? .... 60–65 Letter Shake .... 66–69 Blend Detective 70–75
Standard 5.6 **Level 1: K–2** Understands level-appropriate sight words and vocabulary (e.g., words for persons, places, things, actions; high frequency words such as *said*, *was* and *where*)	Witches' Brew .... 76–77 Bowling for Sight Words .... 78–79 Word-O .... 80–87 Find Your Partner .... 88–89 Fish for Supper .... 90–91 Sight Word Search .... 92–93 Pasta Bowl .... 94–95 Hopscotch .... 96–97 Musical Chairs .... 98–105 Off to School We Go! .... 106–113 Penny Words .... 114–115 Pin the Word on the Donkey .... 116–119 Go Fish .... 120–121 Beat the Clock .... 122–123 Question Game .... 124–129 Follow the Rainbow .... 130–133 It's Raining .... 134–141 Word Roundup 148–153

Ball Toss

Skill:
Identifying Letters

Suggested Group Size:
Whole Class

Activity Overview:
Students identify letters as they toss and catch a ball.

Materials:
- inflatable beach ball
- self-stick Velcro
- 2" x 2" (5 cm x 5 cm) foam pieces
- beach pail

Activity Preparation

1. Write uppercase letters of the alphabet on the foam pieces, one letter per foam piece.

2. Blow up a beach ball.

3. Attach the foam pieces to the ball, using Velcro.

Activity Procedure

1. Have the students sit in a large circle.

2. Place the beach pail in the center of the circle.

3. Toss the ball to a student.

4. Have a student select a letter on the ball and say the name of the letter. If the student correctly identifies the letter, have him or her take the foam piece off the ball and place it in the beach pail. If the student cannot identify the letter, the letter is left on the ball.

5. Have the student toss the ball back to you. Then, toss the ball to another student.

6. Once everyone has had a turn, take each letter out of the pail and have the class read the letters together.

Adaptations

- Write lowercase letters instead of, or in addition to, uppercase letters.
- Have the students close their eyes as they select a letter.
- Write the letters on the ball with a permanent black marker.
- Have the students say the corresponding sound for each letter they select.

Cookie Letters

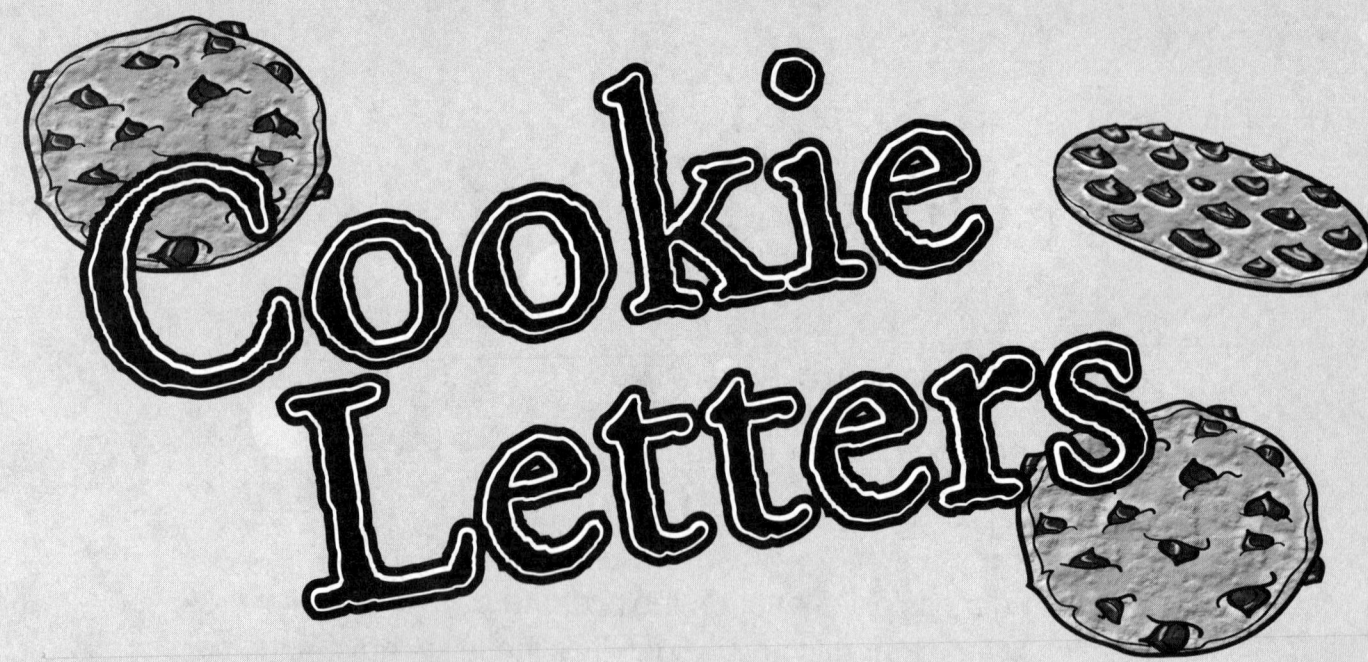

Skill:
Identifying Letters

Suggested Group Size:
2–6 students

Activity Overview:
Students identify letters as they remove letter-shaped cookies from a cookie sheet.

Materials:
- "Cookie Patterns" (page 14)
- cookie sheet
- flat metal spatula
- paper plates, one per student

Activity Preparation

1. Photocopy "Cookie Patterns" onto cardstock paper and color as desired (or print colored copies from the CD). Seven copies of the pattern page are needed to create one cookie for each letter of the alphabet.

2. Cut out the cookies.

3. Write lowercase letters on the backs of the cookies, one letter per cookie.

4. Laminate the cookie patterns for durability.

Activity Procedure

1. Put the cookie patterns, letter side down, on the cookie sheet.

2. Place the cookie sheet in the center of the playing area.

3. Give each child a paper plate.

4. Have a student use the spatula to take a cookie off the cookie sheet.

5. Have the student name the letter on the back of the cookie. If the student correctly identifies the letter, have the student place the cookie on his or her paper plate. If the student cannot identify the letter, have him or her place the cookie back on the cookie sheet.

6. Allow other students to take turns following the same procedure.

7. Once all the cookies have been taken off the cookie sheet, have the students read the letters again as the cookies are placed back on the cookie sheet. The activity is over once all the cookies have been placed back on the cookie sheet.

Adaptations

- Write uppercase letters or sight words on the backs of the cookie patterns.
- Create sunnyside-up eggs instead of cookies (Egg Patterns, page 15). Use a frying pan instead of a cookie sheet.
- Create a poster displaying uppercase letters and have students match the uppercase and lowercase letters by placing the lowercase cookies on the uppercase poster. The shape of the poster could be a giant cookie sheet or frying pan.
- If using words, have students work together to form sentences when the activity is over.
- Create durable cookie pieces out of foam.

Cookie Patterns

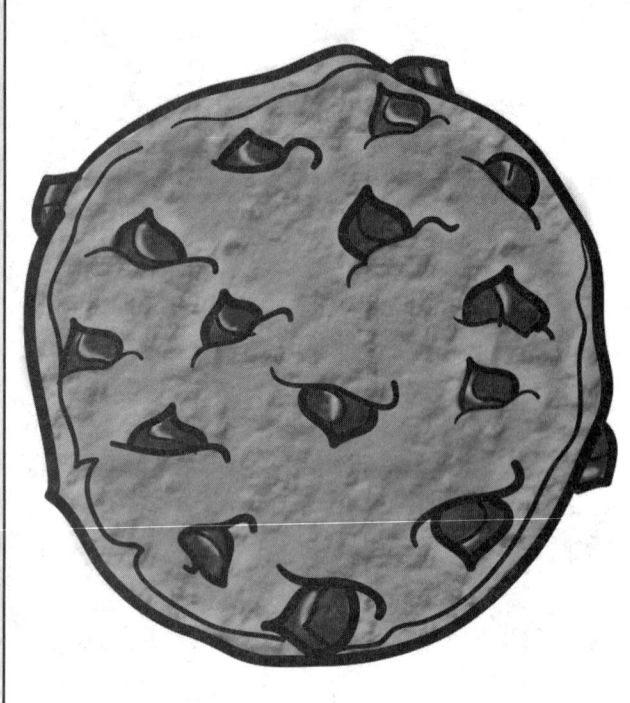
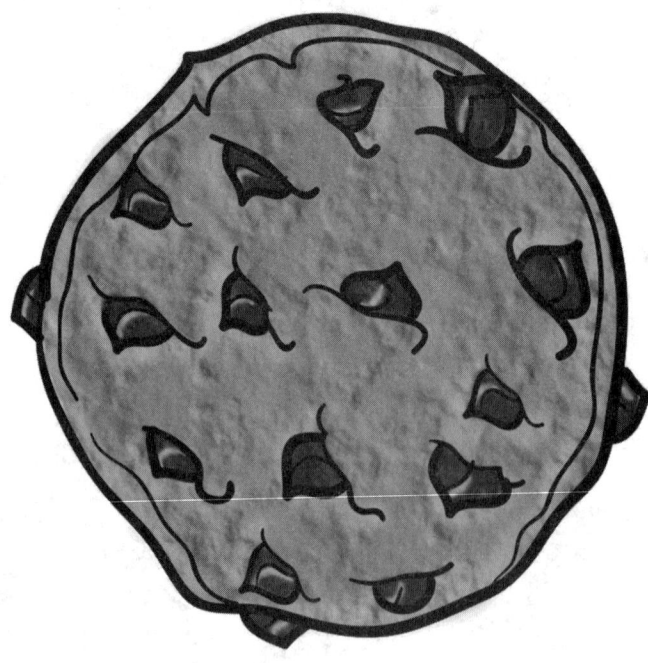
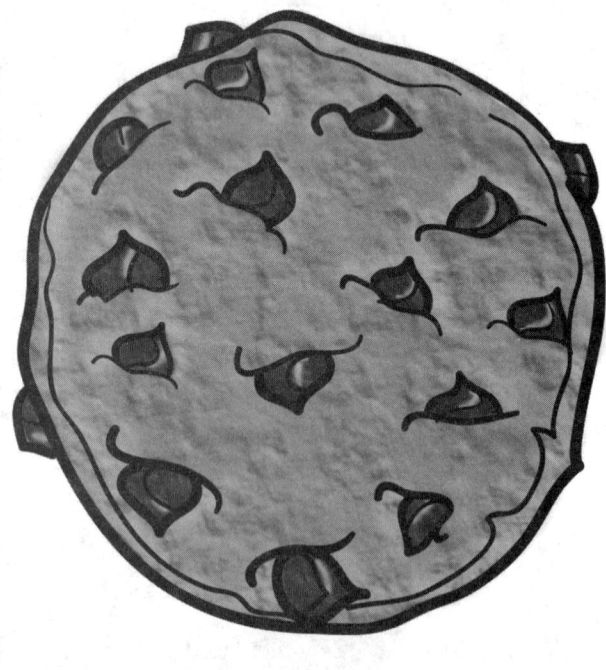
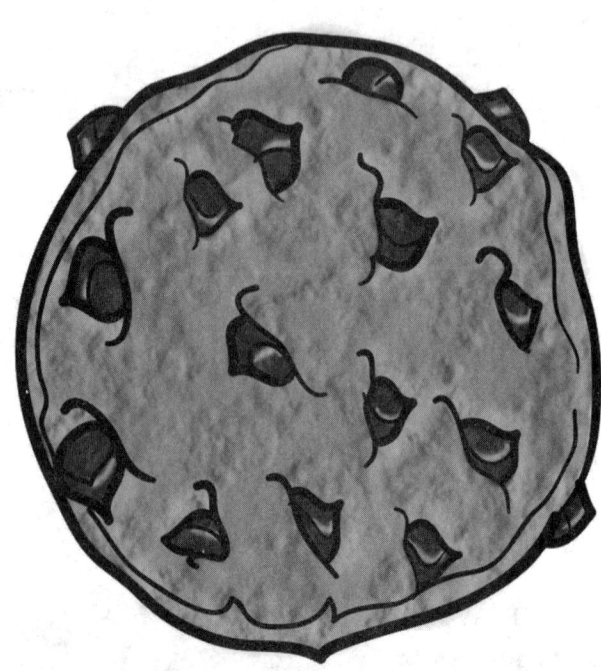

Egg Patterns

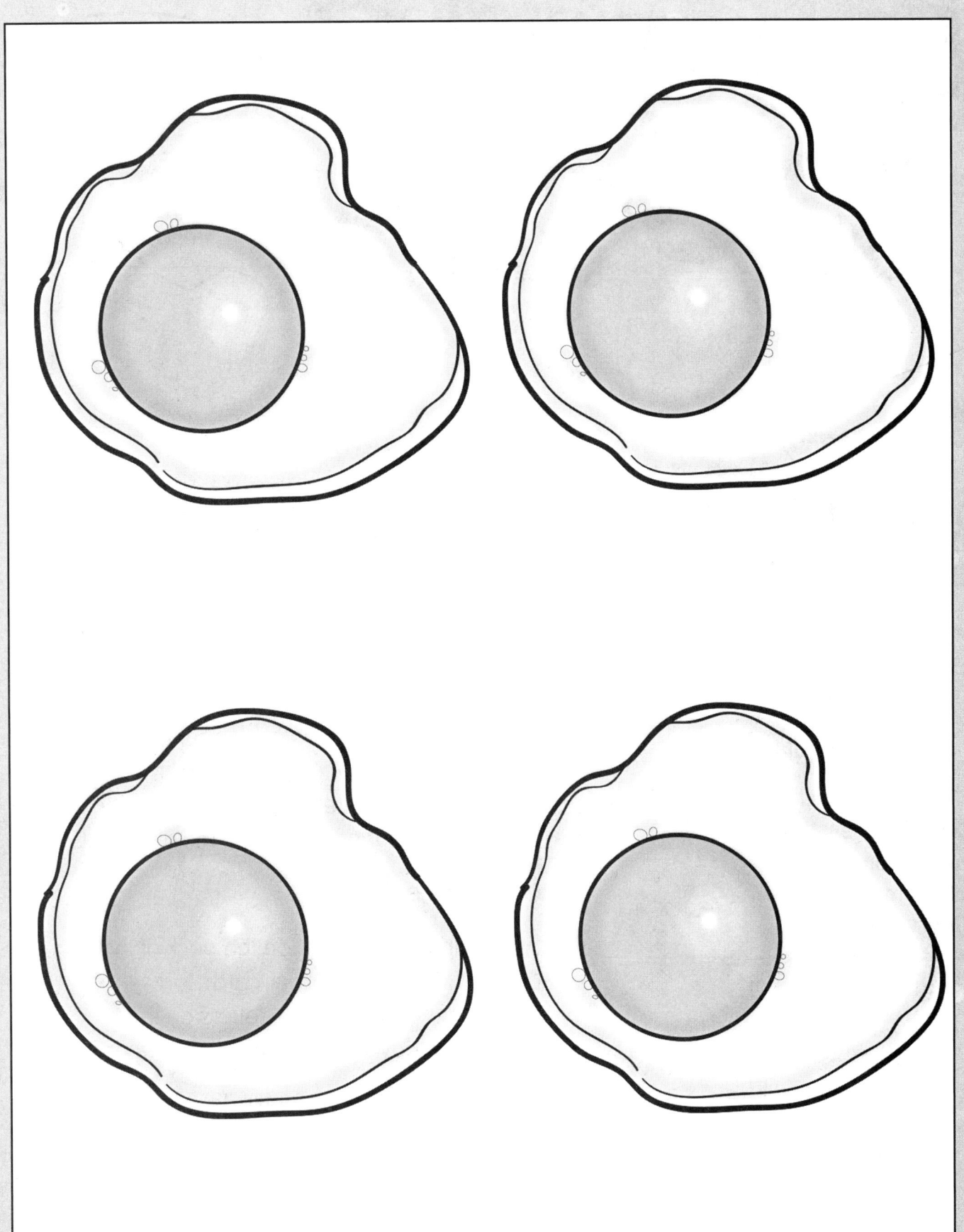

Doggie, Doggie

Skill:
Identifying Letters

Suggested Group Size:
2-4 students

Activity Overview:
Students match uppercase letters on dog-bone cards to lowercase letters on dog-bowl cards.

Materials:
- "Dog Bone Cards" (page 18)
- "Dog Bowl Cards" (page 19)

Activity Preparation

1. Photocopy "Dog Bone Cards" and "Dog Bowl Cards" onto cardstock paper and color as desired (or print color copies from the CD). Five copies of each page are needed to create one for each letter of the alphabet.

2. Cut out the cards.

3. Write uppercase letters on the back of the bone cards, one letter per card. Write the corresponding lowercase letters on the back of the bowl cards, one letter per card.

4. Laminate the cards for durability.

Activity Procedure

1. Spread out the bowl cards on one side of the playing area, with the picture of the dog bowl facing up.

2. Spread out the bone cards on the other side of the playing area with the picture of the dog bone facing up.

3. Have a student turn over one bowl card and one bone card. If the cards have the corresponding upper- and lowercase letters, he can keep the pair of cards. If the upper- and lowercase letters do not correspond, he must turn the cards back over.

4. Have other students take turns following the same procedure. The game is over when all the bones have been matched to the corresponding bowls.

Adaptations

- Have students say the sound the letter makes when they have a match.
- Write sight words instead of letters on the patterns. Write the same words on the backs of the bowl cards as you do on the bone cards. Have students match the sight words.
- Teach students the following song to sing as they play the game.

    Doggie, Doggie
    (To the tune of "Twinkle, Twinkle, Little Star")

    "Doggie, doggie, here's the game.
    Fetch a letter that's the same.
    If you do not find a match,
    Put it back into the batch.
    Doggie, doggie, here's the game.
    Fetch a word that is the same."

Dog Bone Cards

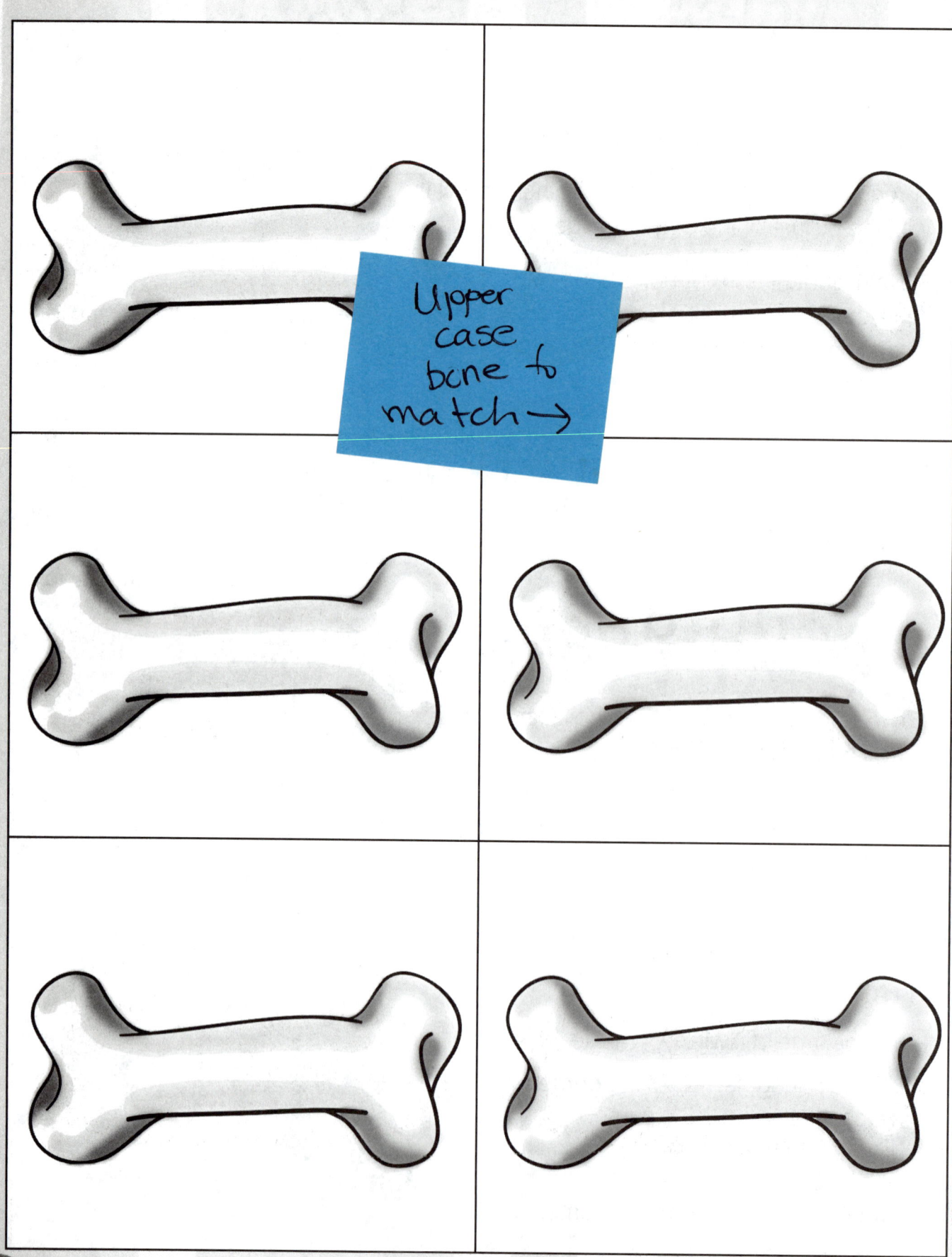

Dog Bowl Cards

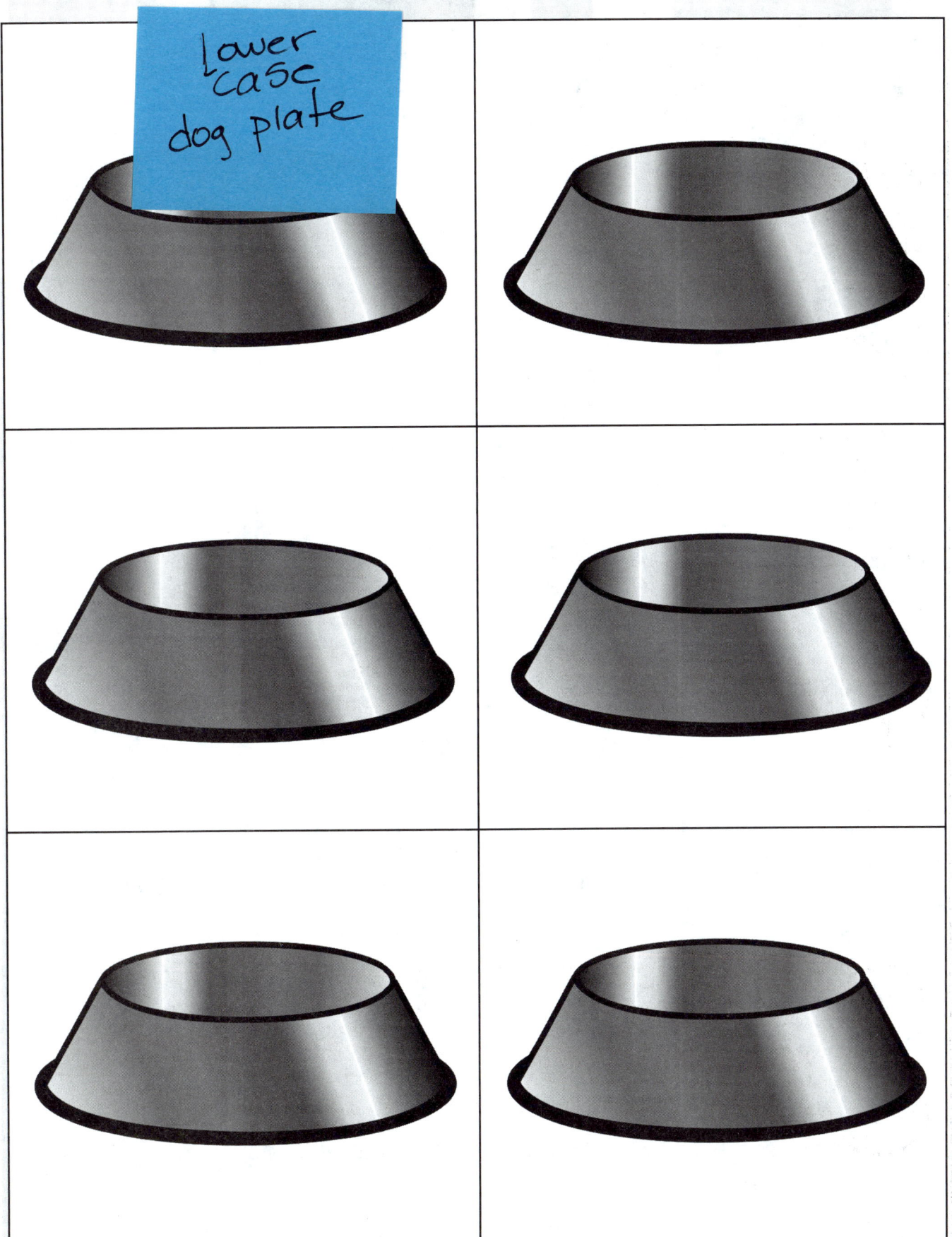

Skill:
Identifying Letters

Letter Walk

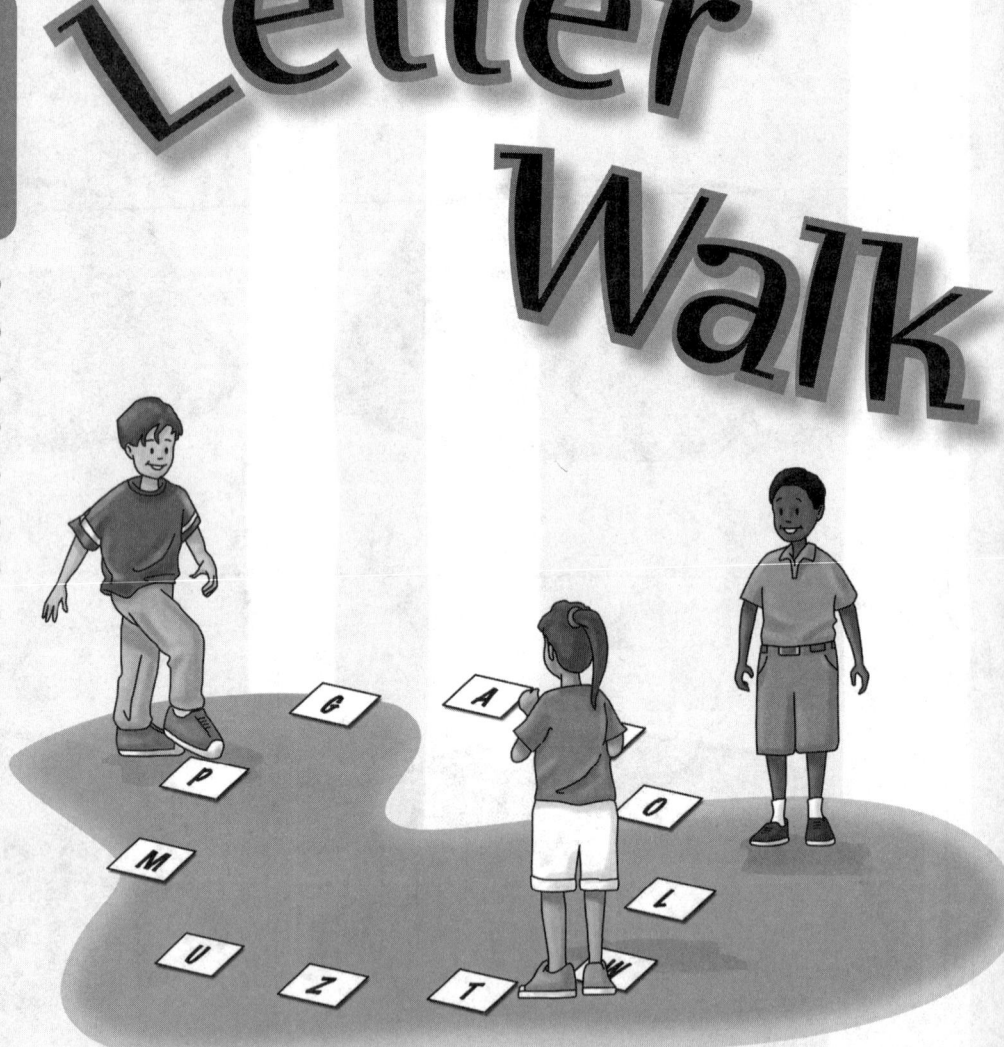

Suggested Group Size:
Whole class

Activity Overview:
Students walk around letters written on cards on the floor as music plays. Once the music stops, a letter is called. The student who is standing next to the called-out letter must say a word that begins with that letter.

Materials:

- 2 sets of "Uppercase Alphabet Cards" (pages 155–161) or "Lowercase Alphabet Cards" (pages 162–168)
- CD player, cassette player, or radio
- music (a CD, tape, or a radio station)

Activity Preparation

1. Photocopy two sets of either the upper- or lowercase alphabet cards (or both, if desired) onto cardstock paper.

2. Cut out the cards.

3. Laminate the cards for durability.

Activity Procedure

1. Place one set of the alphabet cards face up on the floor in a circle. Leave about two feet between each card.

2. Have the students stand by the cards, one student per card.

3. Remove any extra cards from the floor.

4. Remove the same extra letters from the second set of cards so that the letters on the floor match the letters in the second set. This is the set of cards you will be displaying to the children.

5. Shuffle the cards you will be displaying.

6. Play music and instruct the students to walk in a counterclockwise direction.

7. Stop the music at various intervals. When you stop the music, the students must stop walking and stand next to a letter.

8. Take the top card off your deck and display it for the children to see.

9. Have all the students say the name of the letter.

10. Have the student standing next to the corresponding letter say a word that begins with that letter.

11. Continue playing until all letters have been called. If at any time a student has trouble thinking of a word that begins with that letter, he or she may ask a friend for help.

Adaptations

- Have students match uppercase and lowercase letters.
- Identify the names of classmates that begin with the letter displayed.
- Use words instead of letters.
- Have students hop or take baby steps instead of walking while the music plays.

ROCK WALL

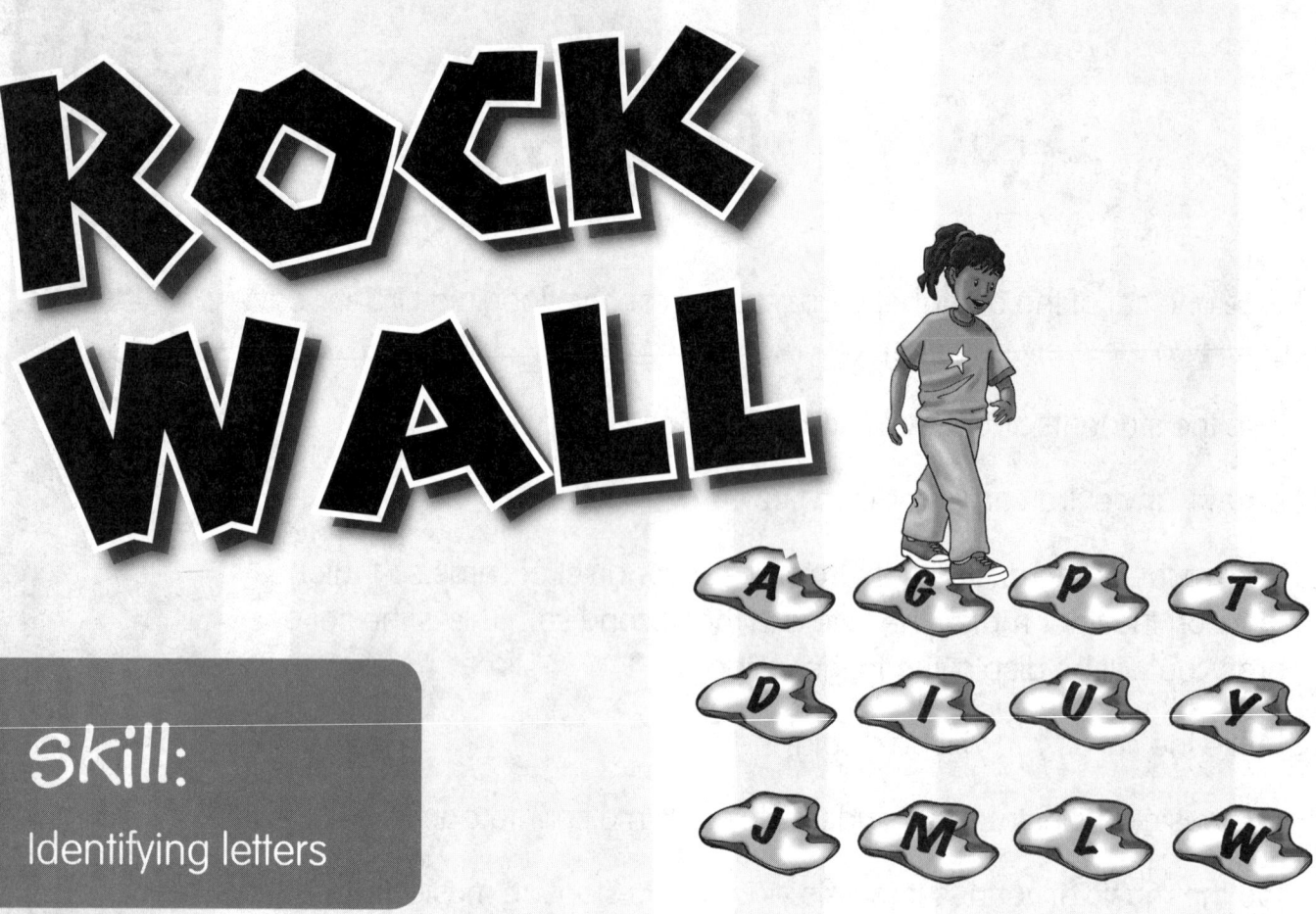

Skill:
Identifying letters

Suggested Group Size:
2–5 students

Activity Overview:
Students identify letters as they climb a rock wall.

Materials:
- brown construction paper
- "Uppercase Alphabet Cards" (pages 155–161) or "Lowercase Alphabet Cards" (pages 162–168)

Activity Preparation

1. Tear or cut brown construction paper into the shape of rocks. You will need 26 rock patterns to create one rock for each letter of the alphabet.

2. Photocopy the alphabet cards onto cardstock paper.

3. Cut out the alphabet cards.

4. Write the letters of the alphabet on the rocks, one letter per rock.

5. Laminate the rocks and cards for durability.

Activity Procedure

1. Line up the students in a row.

2. Place the rocks on the floor in front of the students, creating the same number of rows of rocks as you do students. (Place the rocks in a random order, not alphabetical order.) If you have any odd rocks left over, use these to create a summit.

3. Have the students stand at the base of the rock wall, one student in front of each row of rocks.

4. Stand at the top of the rock wall. Shuffle the alphabet cards.

5. Hold up a letter from the card deck for the first student to see. If the student has that letter "within reach," he or she may step on that rock to begin his climb. "Within reach" means that the rock must be directly in front, or to the left, or right of where he or she is standing. Rocks may not be skipped. Only at the top may students stand on the same rock.

6. Have other students climb the rock wall, following the same procedure.

7. The activity is over once all climbers have reached the top of the rock wall. (Shuffle the alphabet cards and reuse the letters once they have all been shown.)

Adaptations

- Have students say a word that begins with the letter on which they are standing.
- Write words instead of letters on the rocks.
- Allow students to move diagonally.
- Continue the game, having students descend the rock wall once they reach the top.

© Shell Education #50698 Early Childhood Reading Activities

Letter Scoop

Skill:
Identifying letters

Suggested Group Size:
2–6 students

Activity Overview:
Students say the names of the magnetic letters they scoop out of a pail of sand.

Materials:
- magnetic letters
- slotted spoon
- beach pail
- sand

Activity Preparation

1. Pour the sand into a beach pail.
2. Place the magnetic letters in the pail.
3. Stir the magnetic letters into the sand.

Activity Procedure

1. Have a student use the spoon to scoop a magnetic letter out of the sand.

2. Have the student identify the letter that he or she found. If the student can identify the letter, he or she may keep the letter. If the student cannot identify the letter, he or she must put it back into the pail.

3. Have the other students take turns following the same procedure. The activity is over when all the letters have been scooped out of the pail.

Adaptations

- Have the students say the sound the letter makes.
- Have the students think of a word that begins with the letter.
- Write the letters on seashells, one letter per shell. Use the seashells instead of the magnetic letters.
- Have the students put the letters in alphabetical order.
- Have students form words on metal cookie sheets with the magnetic letters.

SMART DRIVERS

Skill:
Identifying letters

Suggested Group Size:
2–5 students

Activity Overview:
Students move their cars along a raceway as they identify letters.

Materials:
- "Smart Drivers" (pages 28–30)
- "Car Game Markers and Game Die" (page 31)

Activity Preparation

1. Photocopy "Smart Drivers" on cardstock paper and color as desired (or print colored copies from the CD).

2. Attach the three game board pages together on the glue tabs to create one large game board.

3. Glue the game board on a piece of poster board for stability.

4. Photocopy "Car Game Markers and Three-Dot Die" onto cardstock paper. Color each car game marker a different color (or print colored copies from the CD).

5. Cut out the game markers.

6. Laminate the game board and game markers for durability.

7. Assemble the game die.

Activity Procedure

1. Place the game board in a central location. Place car game markers at the start of the lanes, one car per lane.

2. Determine which color car each student will use.

3. Have a student roll the die and move his or her car the number of spaces indicated. Once the student lands on a spot, he or she says the name of the letter on which he or she landed. If the student lands on a picture, he or she needs to name the picture and then say the beginning letter of the word.

4. Have other students take turns following the same procedure. The game is over once all players have reached the finish line.

Adaptations

- Use small toy cars as game markers.
- Have students say the name of the letter that comes after the letter on which they landed.
- Have students roll again if they roll a five or a six.
- Have students say a word that begins with the letter on which they land. If they land on a picture, have them name another word that begins with the same letter.

Smart Drivers

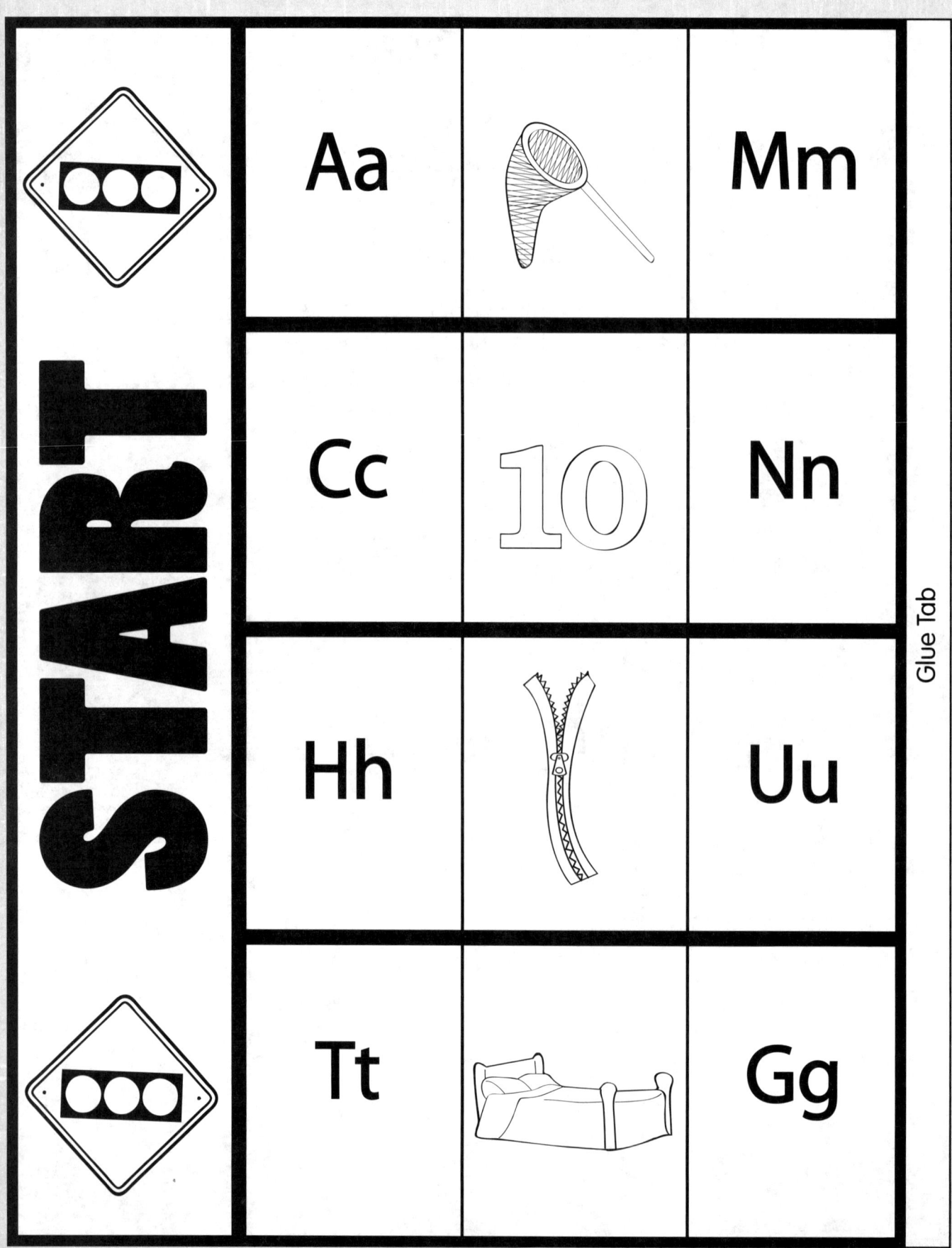

Smart Drivers (cont.)

	Qq	**Bb**	**Tt**
	Ff	**Jj**	**Ll**
	Dd	**Rr**	**Ww**
	Xx	**Pp**	**Kk**

Smart Drivers (cont.)

Smart Drivers Game Markers and Game Die

I'm Going On a Trip

Skill:
Making letter-sound associations

Suggested Group Size:

Whole Class

Activity Overview:

Students name items that begin with the letter displayed on a card for a trip they plan.

Materials:

- "Uppercase Alphabet Cards" (pages 155–161) or "Lowercase Alphabet Cards" (pages 162–168)

Activity Preparation

1. Photocopy the alphabet cards onto cardstock paper.
2. Cut out the cards.
3. Laminate the cards for durability.

Activity Procedure

1. Arrange the students in a circle.

2. Display an alphabet card.

3. Have the first student say, "I'm going on a trip, and I'm going to take a _____." The student must fill in the blank with an item that begins with the same letter as shown on the card.

4. Continue around the circle, displaying a new letter of the alphabet for each student. The game is over when everyone has had a turn.

Adaptations

- Require all the students to suggest an item that begins with the same letter of the alphabet. Do not allow any duplication of items.

- Have each player repeat what those who went before him or her would bring on the trip before a new item is suggested.

- Have students think of an item that ends with the letter shown on the card.

- Play, "I'm Going to the Grocery Store." Have students complete the sentence "I'm going to the grocery store, and I'm going to buy _____." Have students name food items to fill in the blank.

Dinnertime

Skill:
Making letter-sound associations

Suggested Group Size:
2–6 students

Activity Overview:
Students pass a bowl filled with pictures of food and try to determine the initial letter of selected pictures.

Materials:
- "Food Cards" (pages 36–37)
- bowl
- paper plates, one per student

Activity Preparation

1. Photocopy "Food Cards" onto cardstock paper and color as desired (or print colored copies from the CD).

2. Cut out the cards.

3. Write the initial letter of the word on the back of each card.

4. Laminate the cards for durability.

5. Place the cards in the bowl, letter side down.

Activity Procedure

1. Arrange the students in a circle.

2. Provide each student with a paper plate.

3. Have a student select a card from the bowl and say the name of the food pictured.

4. Have the student identify the beginning letter of the word. The student may then look at the other side of the card to confirm his/her answer. If the answer is correct, the student may place the card on his/her paper plate. If the answer is not correct, the student returns the card to the bowl.

5. Have other students take turns following the same procedure. The activity is over when all the food cards are gone.

Adaptations

- Use plastic play food instead of the picture cards.
- Ask the students to identify the ending letters of the words.
- Have the students try to write as many letters as they can on a small whiteboard or other surface for each selected food.
- Teach the students the following song to sing as they play the game:

   Dinnertime

   (To the tune of "This Old Man")

   "Dinnertime, dinnertime,

   Pass the bowl, it's dinnertime!

   Get some food and dig right in,

   Tell me how does it begin?"

Food Cards

Food Cards (cont.)

YUM YOGURT
Strawberry

Free the Animals

Skill:
Making letter-sound associations

Suggested Group Size:
2–5 students

Activity Overview:
Students take pictures of animals from under a basket and determine the initial letter of the selected picture.

Materials:
- "Free the Animals" (pages 40–41)
- "Animal Patterns" (pages 42–43)
- wire basket or container

Activity Preparation

1. Photocopy "Free the Animals" and "Animal Patterns" on cardstock paper and color as desired (or print colored copies from the CD).

2. Attach the two game board pages together on the glue tabs to create one large game board.

3. Cut out the animal patterns.

4. Write the initial letter of each animal on the back of each animal pattern.

5. Laminate the game board and animal patterns for durability.

Activity Procedure

1. Place the game board in the center of the playing area.

2. Put the animal patterns under the wire basket and place next to the game board.

3. Have a student take an animal out from under the basket and say the name of the animal.

4. Have the student identify the beginning letter of that word. Once the student has named the letter, have him or her turn the animal pattern over to confirm the answer.

5. Have the student place the animal card on the game board. The activity continues until all the animals have been set free from the cage.

Adaptations

- Use toy plastic animals instead of the animal patterns.
- Have the students close their eyes as they select an animal.
- Ask the students what letter sound is at the end of each animal's name.
- When setting the animals free, or when putting them back, call out the initial letter of each animal and have the students select the matching animal.

Free the Animals

Free the Animals (cont.)

Animal Patterns

Animal Patterns (cont.)

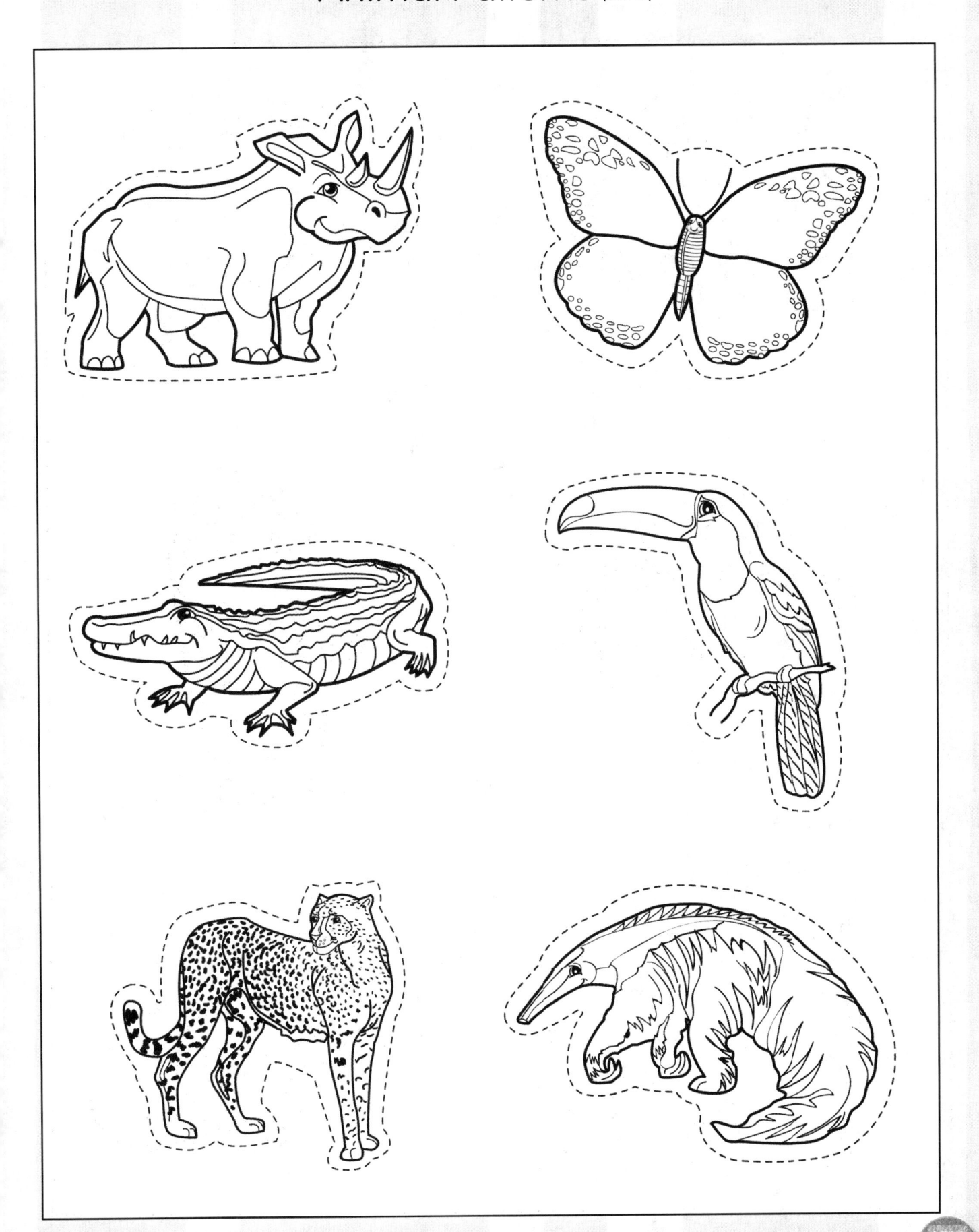

LETTER DETECTIVE

Skill:
Making letter-sound associations

Suggested Group Size:
Whole Class

Activity Overview:
Students search the room to find items that begin with a specific letter.

Materials:
- small white boards (or paper) and markers
- grocery bags

Activity Preparation

1. Determine ahead of time the letter(s) on which you wish to focus. Make sure there are various items in the room that begin with those particular letters.

Activity Procedure

1. Group students into pairs.
2. Provide each pair with a whiteboard, a marker, and a grocery bag.
3. Write a letter on each whiteboard. The same letter can be written on each white board, or you can select a different letter for each pair.
4. Ask each pair of students what sound the letter makes as you write it on the whiteboard.
5. Have the students search the room for items that begin with the letter. Small items may be placed in the grocery bag. Large items may be drawn on the whiteboard. Give the students ample time to find a few items.
6. Gather the class back together to review the items.
7. Have each pair of students share the letter and sound on which they were working and the items they found.

Adaptations

- Divide students into groups of three. The third person can be the one who picks the items up and places them into the bag.
- Have students look for words beginning with blends.
- Use paper instead of white boards. Place the papers on clipboards and later make them into a book.
- Have students look for words that end with a given letter.

Name Game

Skill:
Making letter-sound associations

Suggested Group Size:

Whole Class

Activity Overview:

Students match pictures of classmates to the initial letters.

Materials:
- photographs of the students in the class
- index cards

Activity Preparation

1. Take a picture of each student in your class, or use the photographs provided when school pictures are taken.

2. Print the photographs if necessary.

3. Write the initial letter of each student's name on an index card, one letter per card.

Activity Procedure

1. Place the photographs face down in a central location.

2. Place the index cards with the letters facing up above the photographs

3. Have a student turn a photograph over and say the name of the child pictured.

4. Have the student select an index card that has the corresponding initial letter written on the card. The index card is then placed below the photograph.

5. Follow the same procedure with other students. The activity is over when all the letters have been matched with photographs.

Adaptations

- Write the entire first names of the students instead of just the initial letters.
- Place both the photographs and the letter cards face-down. Have students select a photograph and an index card to see if they match. The activity becomes a memory-type game.
- Include photographs of other people at your school such as the principal, secretary, custodian, and yourself.
- Omit the index cards. Write the initial letter on the back of each photograph. Place the photographs face down on a table, have a student select a photograph, say the letter they see, and guess whose photograph it could be.

Night Sky Match

Skill:
Making letter-sound associations

Suggested Group Size:
2–6 Students

Activity Overview:
Students turn over star pieces that match initial sounds of given pictures.

Materials:
- "Night Sky", one per student (page 50)
- "Star Patterns" (pages 51–54)
- "Night Sky Picture Cards" (pages 55–59)

Activity Preparation

1. Photocopy "Night Sky" and "Night Sky Picture Cards" on cardstock paper and color as desired (or print colored copies from the CD).

2. Photocopy "Star Patterns" on yellow cardstock paper (or print colored copies from the CD).

3. Cut out the stars and picture cards.

4. Laminate the pieces for durability.

Activity Procedure

1. Provide each student with a "Night Sky" game mat.

2. Deal out the stars equally by the number of students playing. Set aside any extra stars that cannot be divided equally.

3. Have the students place the stars on their game mats, letter side up.

4. Hold up the picture cards, one at a time.

5. Have the whole group name the picture and the beginning sound of the word. If a student has a star with the letter that makes the sounds, he or she can turn that star over.

6. The activity continues until all the stars have been turned over.

Adaptations

- Create durable stars out of foam.
- If the student has a letter match, ask him or her to say another word that begins with that letter.
- Include a blank star on each player's board. Besides using picture cards, say the names of planets. If a student can tell you the beginning letter of the planets, he or she may turn the blank star over.
- Write sight words on the blank stars (page 54) and play the game by displaying sight word cards (pages 169–176). Students may turn over their stars if they have the matching word.

Night Sky

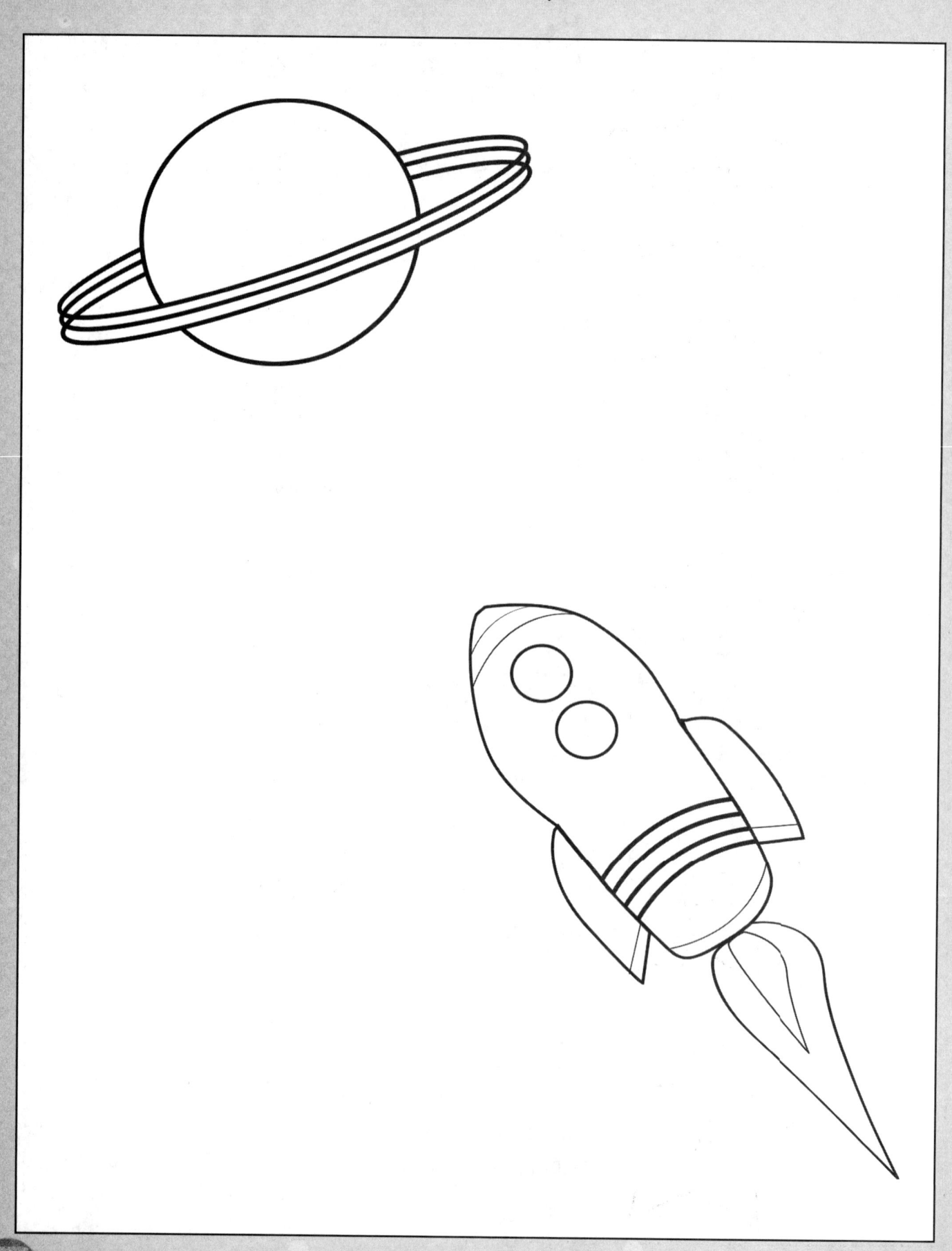

Star Patterns

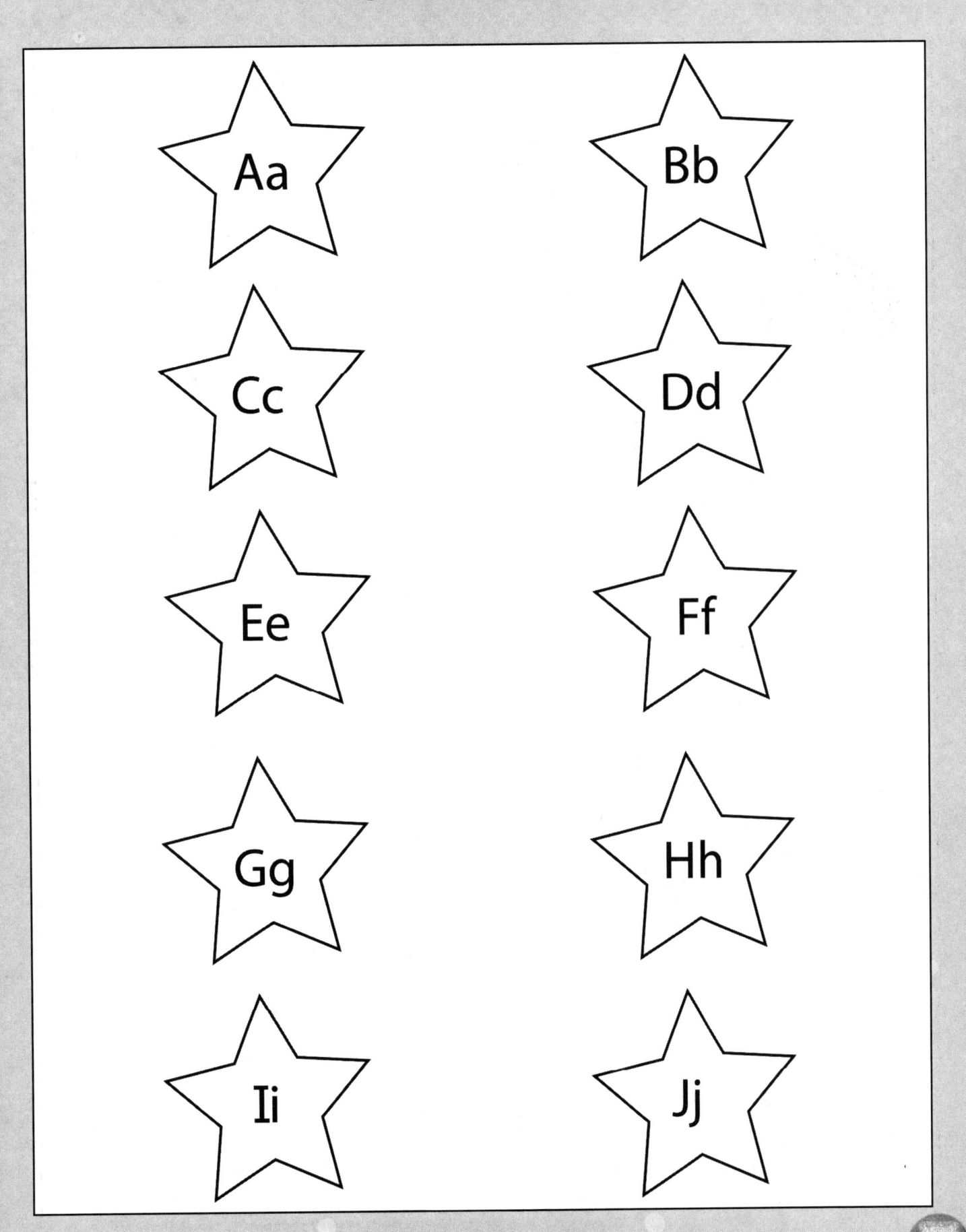

Aa	Bb
Cc	Dd
Ee	Ff
Gg	Hh
Ii	Jj

Star Patterns (cont.)

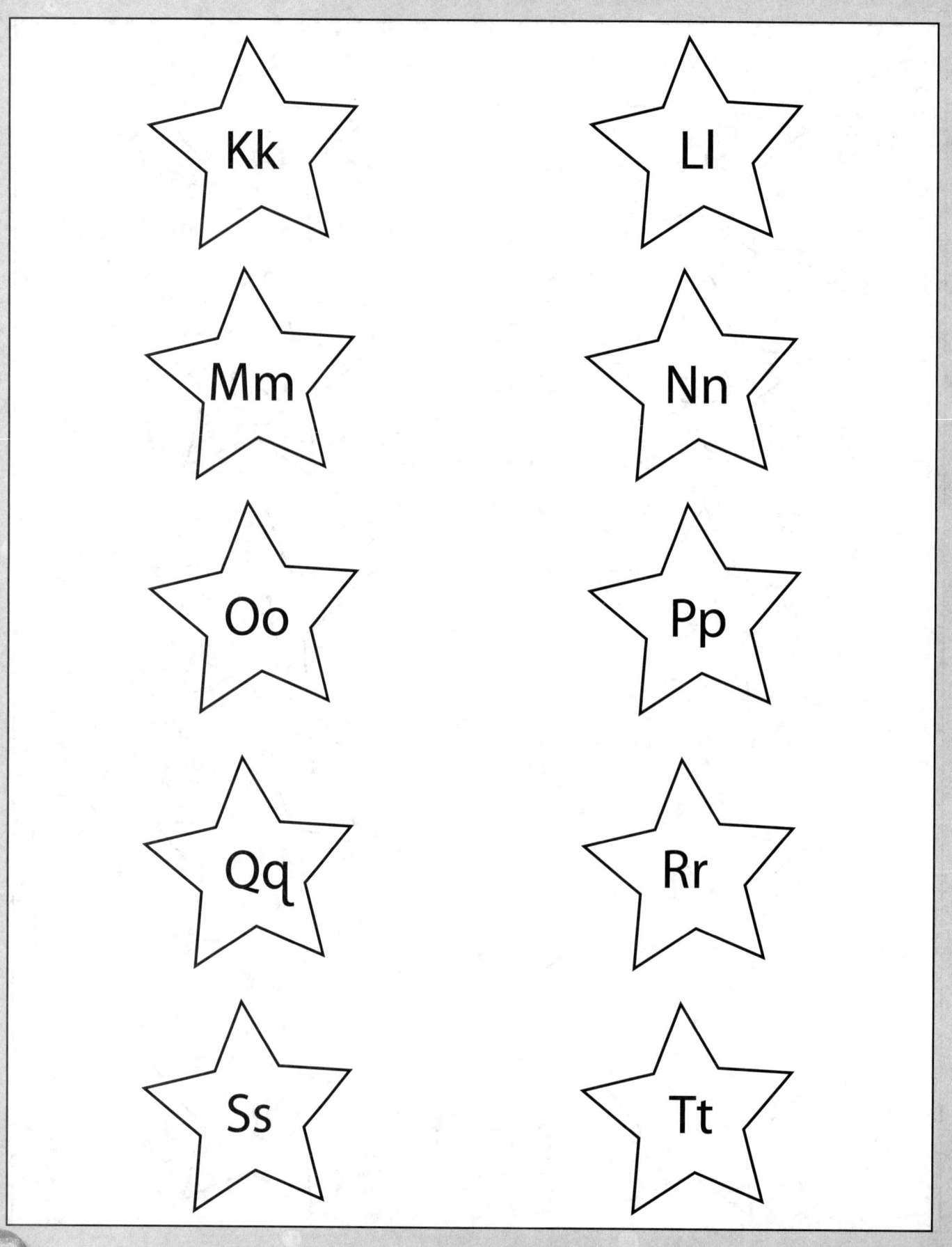

Kk	Ll
Mm	Nn
Oo	Pp
Qq	Rr
Ss	Tt

Star Patterns (cont.)

- Uu
- Vv
- Ww
- Xx
- Yy
- Zz

Star Patterns (cont.)

Night Sky Picture Cards

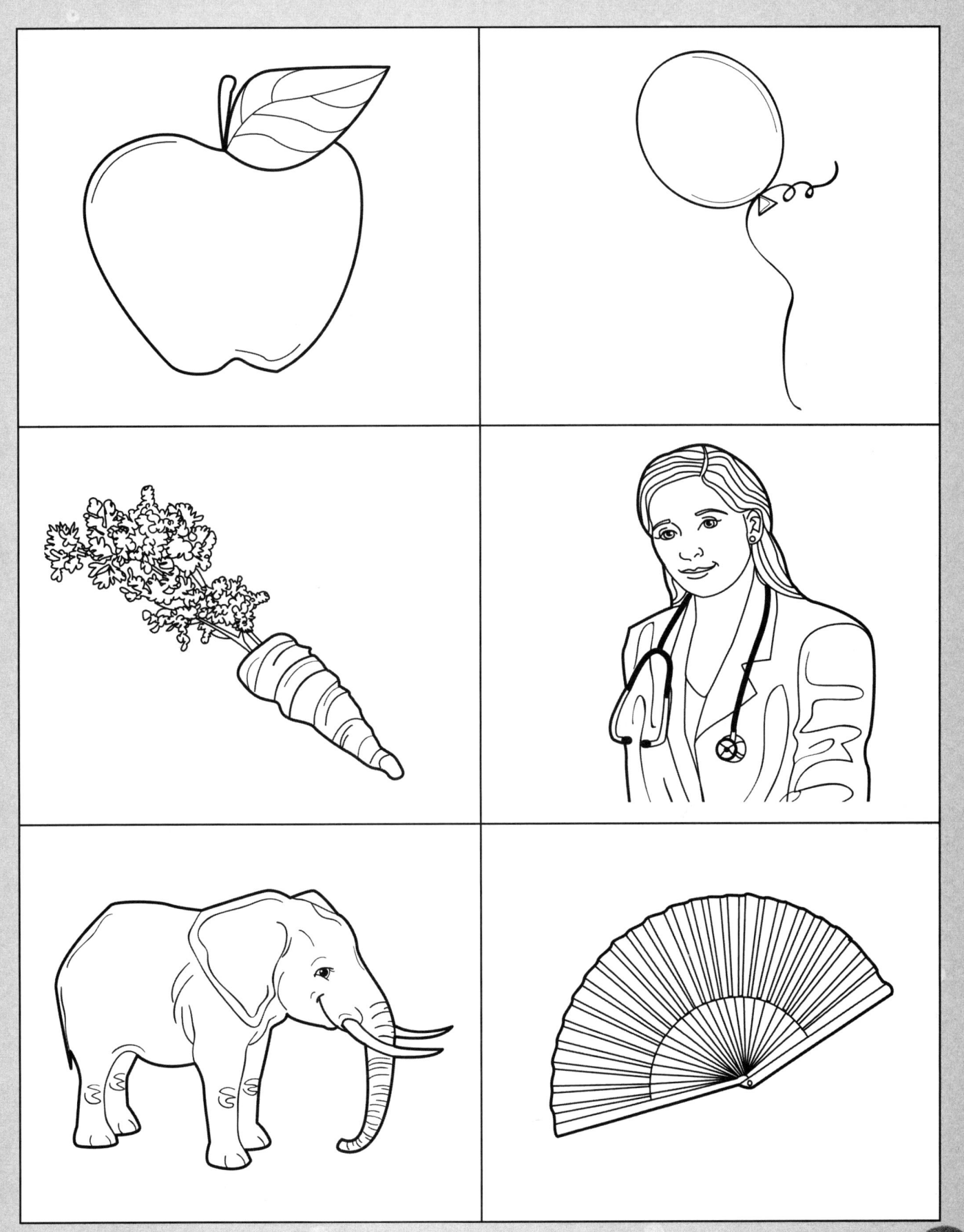

Night Sky Picture Cards (cont.)

56 #50698 Early Childhood Reading Activities © Shell Education

Night Sky Picture Cards (cont.)

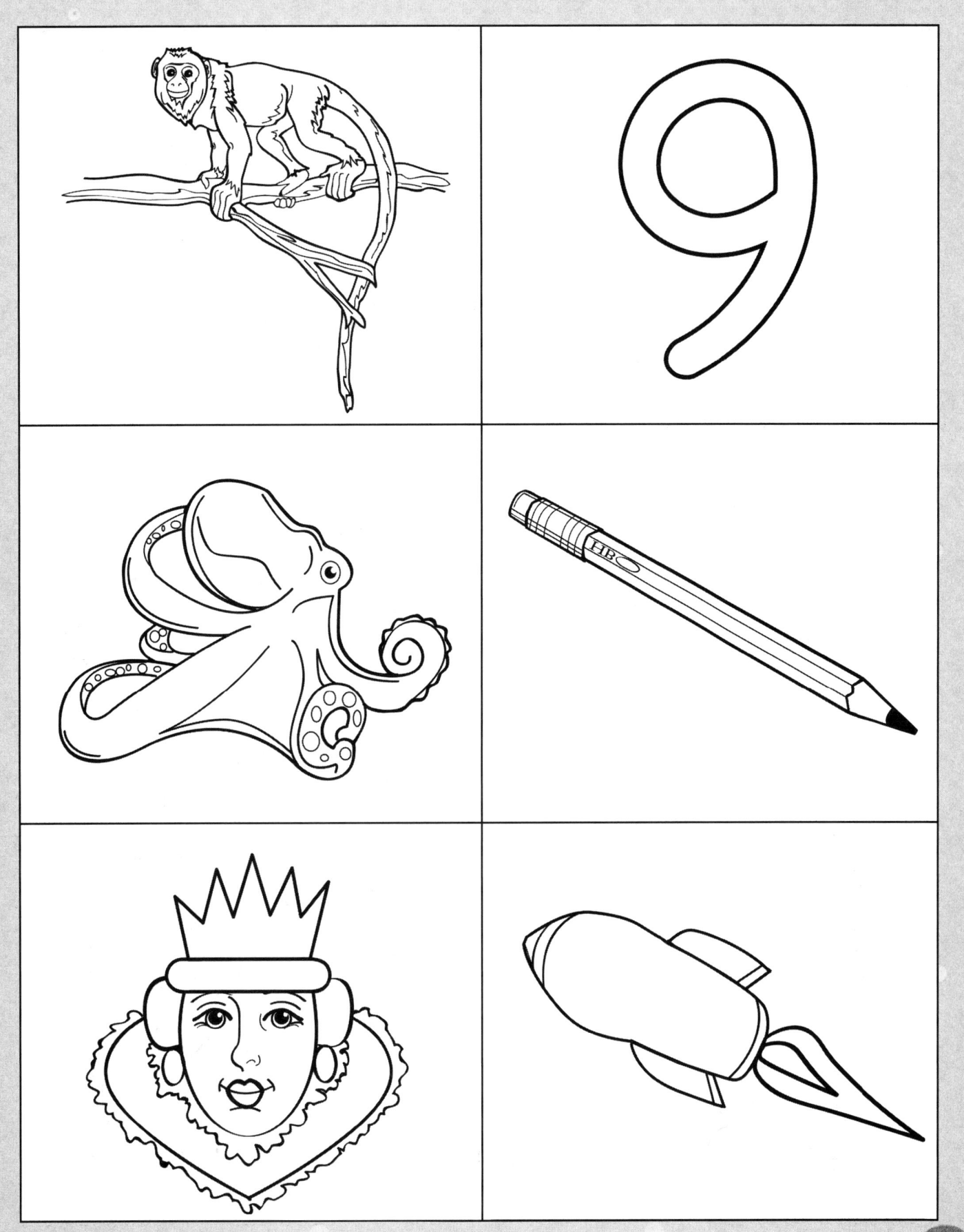

Night Sky Picture Cards (cont.)

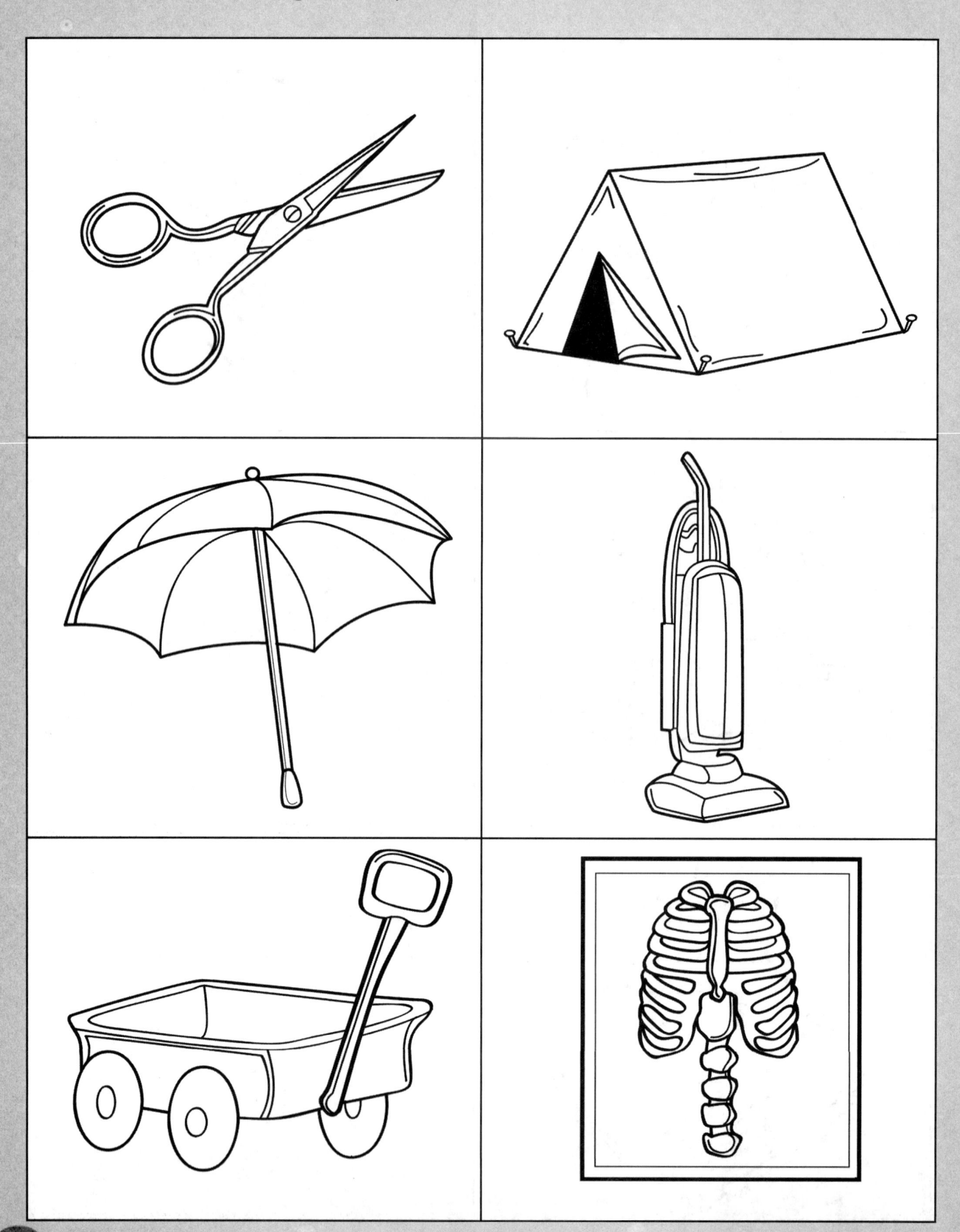

Night Sky Picture Cards (cont.)

What Am I?

Skill:
Making letter-sound associations

Suggested Group Size:
2–4 students

Activity Overview:
Students match initial and ending sound cards to animals.

Materials:
- "Animals Game Mats" (pages 62–65)
- "Uppercase Alphabet Cards" (pages 155–161) or "Lowercase Alphabet Cards" (pages 162–168)
- beans or other game markers, six for each student
- cups or zipper bags, one for each player

Activity Preparation

1. Photocopy "Animals Game Mats" onto cardstock paper and color as desired (or print colored copies from the CD).

2. Photocopy the alphabet cards onto cardstock paper.

3. Cut out the alphabet cards.

4. Select the following letter cards to use in this activity: *a, b, c, d, e, f, g, h, k, l, m, n, p, r, s, t,* and *w*. Set aside the remaining cards.

5. Laminate the game mats and alphabet cards for durability.

6. Place six beans or other game markers in each cup or zipper bag.

Activity Procedure

1. Provide each student with a game mat and a cup of beans.

2. Have the students point to the two boxes within each square on their game mats.

3. Tell the students the first box represents the initial sound of the animal pictured, and the second box represents the ending sound of the animal pictured.

4. Shuffle the alphabet cards and place them in a central location.

5. Have a student turn over the top alphabet card and say the name of the letter and the sound the letter makes.

6. Have the rest of the students look at the pictures on their game mats to see if an animal on their mats begins or ends with that sound. Students can place a bean on the beginning or ending sound box if they have an animal that begins or ends with the sound the letter makes.

7. If a student places a bean on his or her mat, have him or her say the name of the animal out loud for the rest of the group to hear.

8. Have other students take turns turning over alphabet cards, following the same procedure. The activity is over when all the letter cards have been shown.

Adaptations

- Require students to fill only the ending sound box.
- Have the students create their own game mats by drawing other animals or items.
- Clap out the number of syllables of each animal.
- Have the students write the letter for the beginning or ending sound in the correct box.

Animals – Game Mat 1

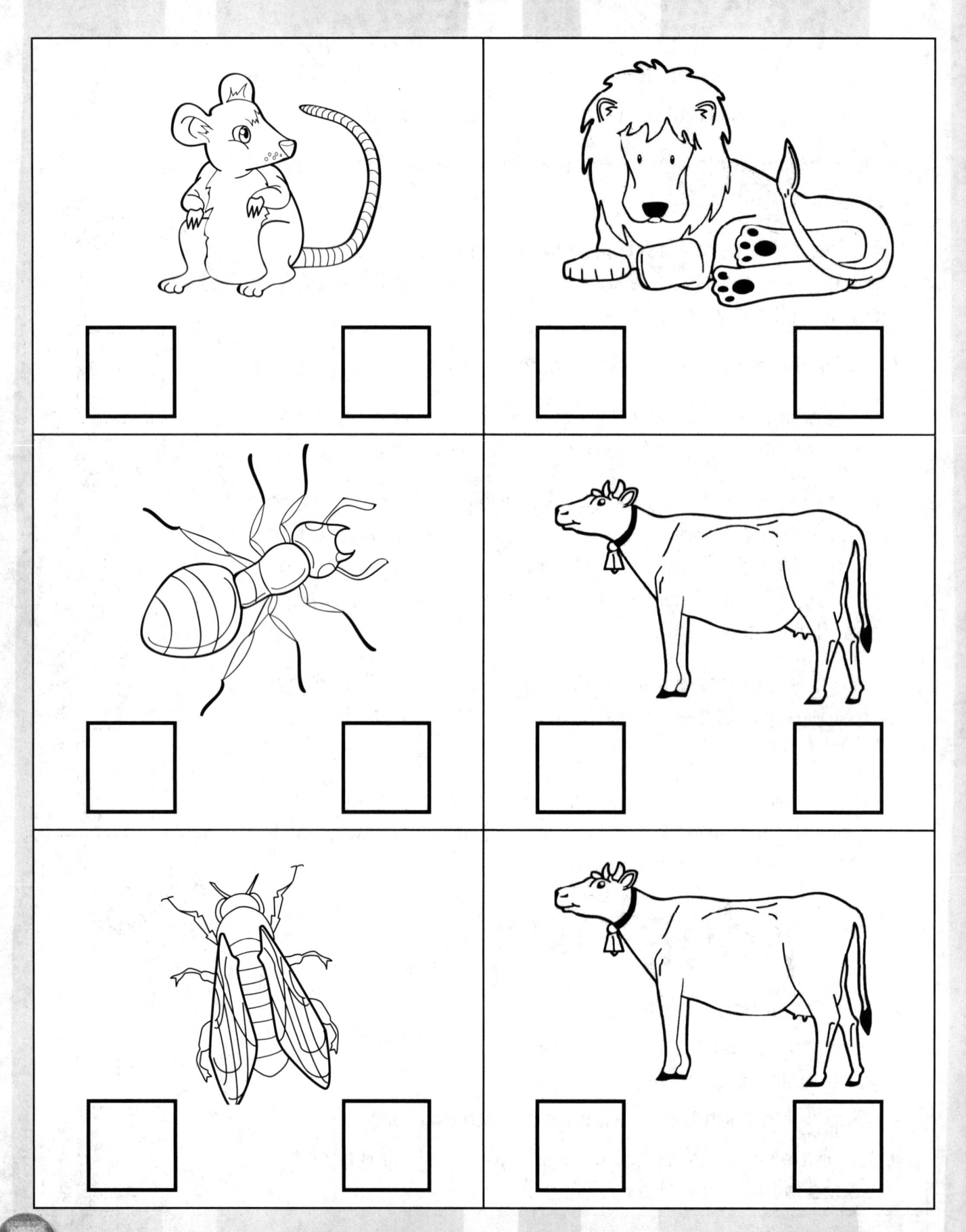

Animals – Game Mat 2

Animals – Game Mat 3

Animals – Game Mat 4

Letter Shake

Skill:
Making letter-sound associations

Suggested Group Size:

2–4 students

Activity Overview:

Students shake an egg carton and identify letters and sounds written in the egg carton compartments.

Materials:

- "Egg Carton Letters" (page 68)
- egg cartons
- a button or other space marker

Activity Preparation

1. Photocopy "Egg Carton Letters" on cardstock paper.

2. Cut out the circles.

3. Determine letters you want students to practice. (You will need 12 letters per egg carton game you create.)

4. Glue the letters inside each compartment of an egg carton, one letter per compartment.

5. Place a button or other space marker in the egg carton and close the lid.

6. Create several egg carton games following the same preparation procedure. Use different letters in each egg carton.

Activity Procedure

1. Provide a student with an egg carton.

2. Have the student shake the egg carton and open the lid.

3. Have the student say the name of the letter that is in the same compartment as the space maker.

4. Ask the student to identify the sound the letter makes.

5. Allow other students to take turns following the same procedure. Continue the game until each student has had five turns, or as time allows.

Adaptations

- Have the students think of a word that begins or ends with the letter.
- Create an egg carton game with "Egg Carton Pictures" (page 69). Have students tell you the word shown on the picture and the letter with which it begins.
- Create an egg carton game with numbers. Have the students identify the numbers.

Egg Carton Letters

Aa Bb Cc Dd Ee
Ff Gg Hh Ii Jj
Kk Ll Mm Nn Oo
Pp Qq Rr Ss Tt
Uu Vv Ww Xx Yy
Zz

Egg Carton Pictures

* Note: The picture for Xx ends with the /ks/ sound.

Blend Detective

Skill:
Making letter-sound associations

Suggested Group Size:
2–5 students

Activity Overview:
Students match initial blends to pictures.

Materials:
- "Blend Detective" (pages 72–73)
- "Initial Blend Cards" (pages 74–75)

Activity Preparation

1. Photocopy "Blend Detective" and "Initial Blend Cards" onto cardstock paper (or print colored copies from the CD).

2. Attach the two game board pages together on the glue tab to create one large game board.

3. Color the pictures on the game mat.

4. Cut out the blend cards.

5. Laminate the game board and blend cards for durability.

Activity Procedure

1. Place the game board in a central location.

2. Place blend cards facedown in a stack in a central location.

3. Tell the students to think about how each picture sounds at the beginning of the word. Point to the pictures on the game board as students name the pictures.

4. Have a student take the top card off the stack of cards and say the sounds in the blend.

5. Have the student find a picture on the game mat with the corresponding initial blend. He or she can place the blend card on top of the picture.

6. Have other students take turns selecting a card and follow the same procedure.

Adaptations

- Have students name other words or items that begin with the same initial blends.
- Have students select a picture, draw it on paper, and write as many letters as they can to name the picture.
- Place on the table actual items represented in the cards and have students determine the initial blends.

Blend Detective

Glue Tab

Blend Detective (cont.)

Initial Blend Cards

br	sw	gl
sl	pr	fr
cl	bl	st

Initial Blend Cards (cont.)

sk	fl	dr
gr	fr	cr
pl	tr	sp

Witches' Brew

Skill:
Reading sight words

Suggested Group Size:
Whole class

Activity Overview:
Students identify letters and read sight words as they scoop the letters out of a cauldron.

Materials:
- magnetic letters
- cookie sheet
- cauldron or large bowl (cauldrons are available at party stores, in the Halloween section)
- ladle

Activity Preparation

1. Determine a sight word you want students to practice.

2. Place magnetic letters that spell the sight word into the cauldron.

Activity Procedure

1. Select a student to sit next to you in front of the class. Give the cauldron and ladle to the student. Hold a cookie sheet for students to see.

2. Give the ladle to the student and have him or her stir the letters around in the cauldron. As the student scoops a letter out of the cauldron, have him or her place it on the cookie sheet. The student then says what the letter is. The process continues until all the letters have been placed on the cookie sheet.

3. Have the student rearrange the letters so that they form a word.

4. Have the rest of the class read the word.

5. Give turns to other students. Limit the activity to three turns or fewer per day. Keep track of who has had a turn.

Adaptations

- Use magnetic words to create a short sentence.
- Teach students the following songs to sing as the cauldron is stirred.
  (To the tune of "This Old Man")

    "Witches' brew,

    Witches' brew,

    Stir to make a Halloween stew.

    Stir it fast,

    Stir it slow,

    Now say all the letters that you know."

- Sing this song if a student needs help with a letter. Allow another student to help identify the letter.
  (To the tune of "Farmer in the Dell")

    "The witch needs a cat,

    The witch needs a cat,

    To ask the witch, 'Which letter is that?'"

Bowling for Sight Words

Skill:
Reading sight words

Suggested Group Size:
2–4 students

Activity Overview:
Students knock down "bowling pins" and then practice reading the words on the pins.

Materials:
- "Sight Word Cards" (pages 169–176)
- 10 empty water bottles
- sand (playground sand is available at home-improvement stores)
- a ball
- masking tape

Activity Preparation

1. Photocopy "Sight Word Cards" on cardstock paper.

2. Cut out the cards.

3. Fill the empty water bottles one-quarter full of sand. (Be sure to tighten the cap.)

4. Determine ten sight words for students to practice reading.

5. Tape the sight word cards on the front of the water bottles, one word per bottle.

Activity Procedure

1. Set the water bottles up in a bowling pin configuration.

2. Determine a starting line and place a piece of masking tape on the floor as a marker.

3. Tell students that the goal is to knock down as many "pins" as possible with a ball.

4. Have a student stand behind the starting line and roll the ball toward the pins. The student must read the sight words on the pins he or she knocked down.

5. Return the pins to the bowling pin configuration.

6. The game is over when each student has had three chances to knock down pins or as time allows.

Adaptations

- Use the letter cards (pages 155–168) instead of sight word cards.
- Have all the students in the group read the sight words as the bowler holds up the pins.
- Allow the bowler two rolls in order to try to knock down more pins.
- Use a larger or smaller ball to make the task easier or more challenging.

Word-O

Skill:
Reading sight words

Suggested Group Size:
2–5 students

Activity Overview:
Students practice reading sight words as they play bingo.

Materials:
- "Word-O Cards" (pages 82–86), one per student
- "Sight Word Cards" (pages 169–176)
- beans or other space markers, 20 per student
- cups or plastic zipper bags, one per student

Activity Preparation

1. Photocopy "Word-O Cards" on cardstock paper and color as desired (or print colored copies from the CD).

2. Photocopy "Sight Word Cards" on cardstock paper.

3. Cut out the cards.

4. Laminate the cards for durability.

5. Place beans or other space markers in the cups or plastic zipper bags.

Activity Procedure

1. Give each student a Word-O Card and a cup or bag of space markers.

2. Display one sight word card at a time.

3. Have the students read the sight word out loud and then check to see if the word is on any of their cards. If they have the word, they can place a space marker on the box containing that word.

4. Once all the words on a card have space markers on them, the student may say, "Word-O."

5. Continue to play until everyone has covered all the spaces on his or her Word-O Card.

Adaptations

- Require only five spaces to be covered in a row across, down, or diagonally.
- Say a word that rhymes with the sight words on the cards rather than displaying the sight word cards. Students can put a space marker on any sight word that rhymes with the word called.
- Have students say words that rhyme with the sight words.
- Photocopy the blank card (page 87) and create your own Word-O Cards using other sight words or letters.

Word-O Card 1

she	same	his	had	of
but	said	you	as	I
this	on	and	went	all
there	it	can	with	from
out	was	at	we	in

Word-O Card 2

be	said	in	one	for
we	that	an	they	this
of	had	all	are	to
went	at	same	on	your
is	were	by	how	have

Word-O Card 3

his	went	on	what	this
some	up	one	he	I
and	but	can	is	a
were	be	to	an	as
your	that	the	from	or

Word-O Card 4

your	all	up	one	the
was	out	and	have	at
to	his	how	or	are
there	can	but	when	it
with	what	in	for	that

Word-O Card 5

in	but	was	when	is
for	with	as	by	or
up	said	of	there	we
the	are	from	he	an
they	how	out	be	I

Blank Word-O Card

Find Your Partner

Skill:
Reading sight words

Suggested Group Size:
Whole class

Activity Overview:
Students look for the classmate who has the same sight word as they do.

Materials:
- "Sight Word Cards" (pages 169–176)

Activity Preparation

1. Photocopy two sets of "Sight Word Cards" on cardstock paper.

2. Determine the words you will use and create matching sets of cards so that you have two of each word.

Activity Procedure

1. Display the sight word cards to the students. Have the students practice reading the cards as you show them.

2. Shuffle the cards.

3. Distribute the cards, one per student. Tell students not to show their words to anyone yet.

4. Have students get up and compare words with one another in order to find their partners. When a student finds his or her partner (one who has the same word as he or she does), both sit down together in another part of the room, away from the walking, talking classmates.

5. Once everyone has found his or her partner, have each pair show their matching cards and say the words on them.

Adaptations

- Have students use their cards to create simple sentences.
- Use the uppercase and lowercase letter cards (pages 155–168). Have students match uppercase letters to lowercase letters.
- Write color words on one set of cards and mark the other cards with the actual colors.
- Write number words on one set of cards and write the corresponding numerals on the other set of cards.

Fish for Supper

Skill:
Reading sight words

Suggested Group Size:
2–6 students

Activity Overview:
Students practice reading sight words as they go fishing.

Materials:
- "Sight Word Cards" (pages 169–176)
- magnetic bingo wand
- magnetic bingo chips

Activity Preparation

1. Photocopy the sight word cards.
2. Cut out the sight word cards.
3. Laminate the cards for durability.
4. Glue the magnetic bingo chips onto the backs of the sight word cards.

Activity Procedure

1. Place the sight word cards in the center of the playing area.

2. Have a student use the magnetic wand to pick up a sight word card.

3. Have the student read the word on the card. If the student reads the word correctly, he or she may keep the card. If the student cannot read the word, the card is placed back with the rest of the cards.

4. Have students take turns following the same procedure until all the cards are gone. Continue the activity, if desired, by having students read the words again as they place the cards back onto the table.

Adaptations

- Write the sight words on fish patterns.
- Have students work together to form sentences using the words.
- Have students name words that rhyme with the words on the fish they catch.
- Use letters instead of words on the fish.

Sight Word Search

Skill:
Reading sight words

Suggested Group Size:
2–4 Students

Activity Overview:
Students locate sight words in newspapers and magazines.

Materials:
- construction paper, one sheet per student
- glue, one bottle per student
- scissors, one pair per student
- magazines and newspapers

Activity Preparation

1. Review the magazines and newspapers. Remove any content that may be inappropriate for children. Children's magazines work well for this activity.

Activity Procedure

1. Place the magazines and newspapers in a central location.

2. Provide each student with a piece of construction paper, scissors, and a bottle of glue.

3. Tell students to look through the magazines and newspapers in search of sight words they can read.

4. Have them cut out the sight word and glue it to the piece of construction paper.

5. Require students to find 20 sight words.

6. Have students practice reading one another's sight words.

Adaptations

- Increase or decrease the number of sight words students must find.
- Create a poster listing sight words you want students to locate.
- Have students arrange the sight words to form simple sentences.
- Have students find letters or numbers.

Pasta Bowl

that *was* *some*

Skill:
Reading sight words

Suggested Group Size:
2–6 students

Activity Overview:
Students practice reading sight words as they scoop pasta with words written on them.

Materials:
- large pieces of dried uncooked pasta (such as ziti)
- a large bowl
- paper plates, one per student
- a ladle
- a permanent black marker

Activity Preparation

1. Write sight words on the dried pasta.
2. Place the pasta in the bowl.

Activity Procedure

1. Place the pasta bowl and ladle in a central location.

2. Provide each student with a paper plate.

3. Have a student use the ladle to scoop out a piece of pasta. The student reads the sight word on the pasta. He or she can place the piece of pasta on his or her plate if the word is read correctly. If the word is not read correctly, he or she must return the piece of pasta to the bowl.

4. Have other students take turns following the same procedure. The activity is over when all the pasta has been scooped out of the bowl.

Adaptations

- Have the rest of the group try to spell the sight words.
- Have students scoop out several pieces of pasta. Have them try to form a sentence with the words.
- Write letters instead of words on the pasta. Have students say another word that begins with the same letter.

Hopscotch

Skill: Reading sight words

Suggested Group Size:
2–3 students

Activity Overview:
Students will practice reading sight words as they hop their way down a hopscotch board.

Materials:
- "Sight Word Cards" (pages 169–176)
- hopscotch board
- beanbags (or another type of space marker if bean bags are not available)

Activity Preparation

1. Photocopy "Sight Word Cards" on cardstock paper.
2. Cut out the cards.
3. Laminate the cards for durability.
4. Prepare a hopscotch board. You may draw one on the ground, or use tape to create one on the carpet.
5. Without covering the numbers on the hopscotch board, place the word cards in each square. Several index cards may be placed in each square.

Activity Procedure

1. Have a student toss a beanbag onto the number-one box on the hopscotch board. The student hops down the hopscotch board by hopping in each square. On the way down the hopscotch board, the student must pick up a word card from the box containing the beanbag. The student must then skip that number by jumping over the square. Note: Some young children may not yet be able to hop on one foot. Allow these children to participate by jumping with two feet in each square.

2. Once the student has reached the end of the hopscotch board, he or she returns to the beginning by once again hopping on each square. When the student reaches the beanbag, he or she picks it up and proceeds to the beginning of the hopscotch board. Once the student gets back to the beginning, he or she reads the word on the card and gives the card to the teacher.

3. Have other students take turns following the same procedure. Once all the students have successfully completed square one, proceed with the game by having the students toss the beanbag onto the second square, then the third square, and so on. The game is over when each student has read 10 words.

Adaptations

- Use a rubber mat or commercially prepared hopscotch board.
- Use the uppercase or lowercase letter cards (pages 155-168) instead of the word cards.
- If using letter cards, have students say a word that begins with that letter.
- Create a shorter or longer hopscotch board.

Musical Chairs

Skill:
Reading Sight Words

Suggested Group Size:
Whole class

Activity Overview:
While music plays, students walk around a group of chairs that have words taped to them. Once the music stops, they kneel in front of a chair to see if they have the matching word that was called.

Materials:
- "Sight Word Cards" (pages 169–176)
- chairs, one per student
- music (CD player or radio)

Activity Preparation

1. Photocopy two sets of "Sight Word Cards" on cardstock paper.

2. Cut out the cards.

3. Laminate the cards for durability.

4. Set out the same number of chairs as students.

5. Arrange chairs back-to-back in two rows.

6. Tape the sight word cards from one set to the inside backs of the chairs. Set aside any unused word cards.

7. Remove the same unused word cards from the second set of cards so that the second set of cards contains the same words that are taped on the chairs.

Activity Procedure

1. Have each student stand in front of a chair.

2. Explain that each chair has a different word taped to it.

3. Tell the students to look at the word that is taped on the chair in front of them.

4. Explain that you will play music, and that when the music stops they will need to kneel in front of a chair that is close to them. (Model how to kneel, if necessary.)

5. Play the music for 10–15 seconds and then stop it. Monitor the students as they kneel down in front of a chair. If two students both go to the same chair, you make the decision who stays and who needs to find another chair.

6. Select a sight word from your deck of cards and ask the students to read it. The student who has that word on his/her chair gets to sit on the chair and take a rest. Put that card off to the side so that you do not use it again.

7. Have the other players stand up and resume walking as you restart the music.

8. Continue the game until everyone is sitting on a chair.

Adaptations

- Use letter cards (pages 155–168) instead of words cards.
- Place pictures on the chairs. Hold up a letter card. Students who have a picture that begins with that letter get to sit down.
- Instead of having the students walk as the music plays, have them take baby steps or giant steps.
- Use "Musical Rhyming Cards" (pages 100–105). A student may sit down if the sight word on his or her chair rhymes with the picture card shown.

Musical Rhyming Cards

100 #50698 Early Childhood Reading Activities © Shell Education

Musical Rhyming Cards (cont.)

Musical Rhyming Cards (cont.)

Musical Rhyming Cards (cont.)

Musical Rhyming Cards (cont.)

Musical Rhyming Cards (cont.)

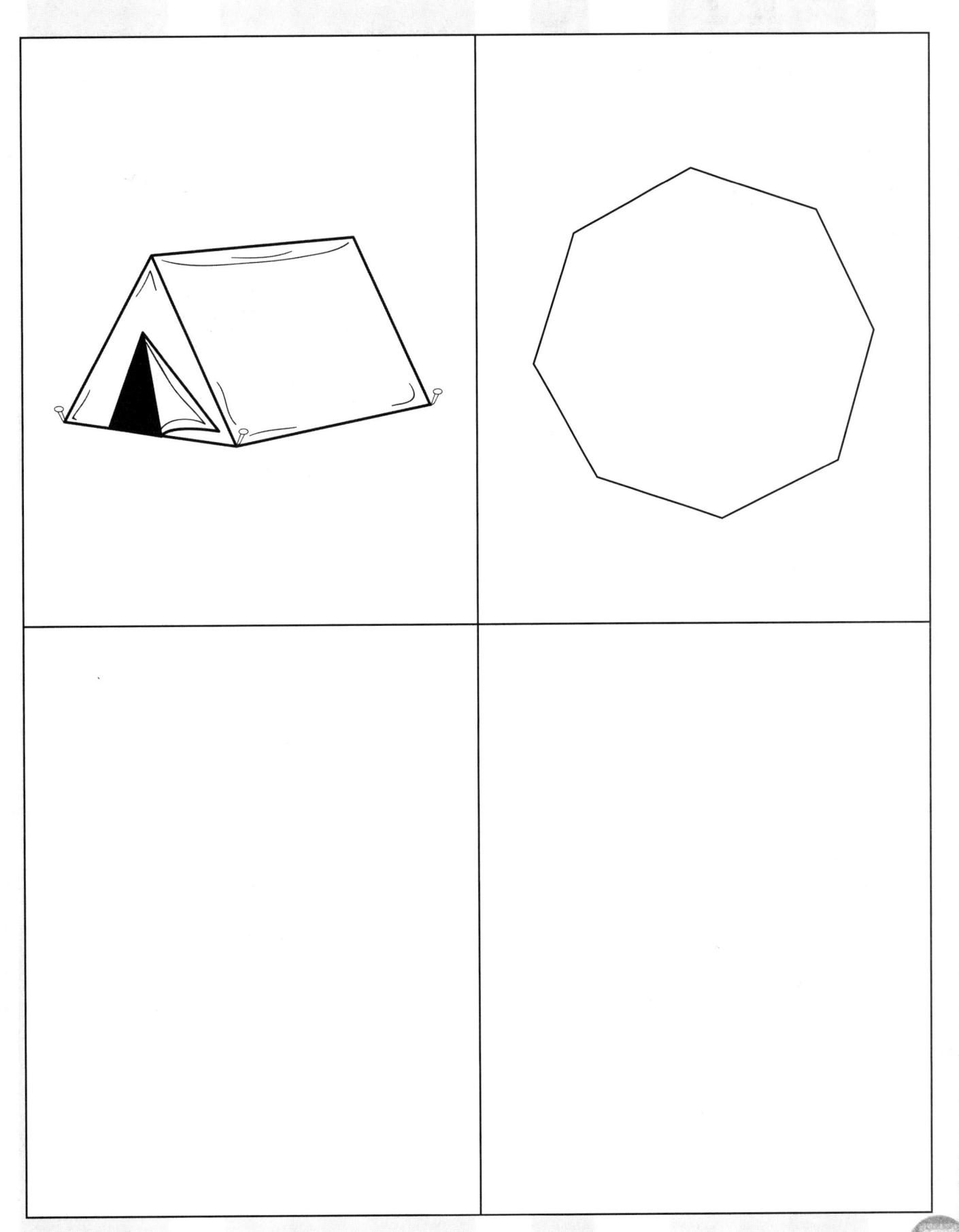

Off to School We Go!

Skill:
Reading sight words

Suggested Group Size:
2–4 students

Activity Overview:
Students follow a path to school as they collect letters to make sight words.

Materials:
- "Off to School We Go!" (pages 108–109)
- "Off to School We Go! Letter Cards" (pages 110–113)
- "Uppercase Letter Cards" (pages 155–161) or "Lowercase Letter Cards" (pages 162–168)
- space markers (such as buttons or beans)
- die

Activity Preparation

1. Photocopy "Off to School We Go!" on cardstock paper and color as desired (or print colored copies from the CD).

2. Attach the two game board pages together on the glue tab to create one large game board.

3. Photocopy "Uppercase Letter Cards" or "Lowercase Letter Cards" on cardstock paper and cut out the cards.

4. Laminate the game board and letter cards for durability.

Activity Procedure

1. Place the game board in a central location.

2. Arrange the letter cards in alphabetical order with the letters facing up next to the game mat.

3. Have students place their space markers on the house.

4. Have a student roll the die. If he or she rolls a one, two, three, or four, he or she can move his or her space marker the corresponding number of spaces. If the student can read the word, he or she can collect the letters that form that word. Have the student place the word in front of his or her playing area. If a five or six is rolled, the player must to go back to the beginning of the game.

5. Have other players take turns following the same procedure. The game is over once everyone has reached the school.

Adaptations

- Use magnetic letters instead of letter cards. Have students form their words on cookie sheets.

- If a student rolls a five or six, let him or her move his or her space marker the corresponding number of spaces.

- At the end of the game, have students work together to form a sentence using some of the words.

- Have students say words that rhyme with the sight words.

Off to School We Go!

Off to School

play like can

look little big

see

do you are went

Glue Tab

Off to School We Go! (cont.)

We Go

we · he · she · my · boy · girl · love · so · get · to

Off to School We Go! Letter Cards

a	a	a	b
b	c	d	e
e	e	e	e
e	e	e	e
e	e	g	g

Off to School We Go! Letter Cards (cont.)

g	h	h	i
i	i	i	k
k	l	l	l
l	l	l	l
m	n	n	o

Off to School We Go! Letter Cards (cont.)

o	o	o	o
o	o	o	p
r	r	s	s
s	t	t	t
t	t	u	v

Off to School We Go! Letter Cards (cont.)

w	w	y	y
y	y		

Penny Words

Skill:
Reading sight words

Suggested Group Size:
2–6 students

Activity Overview:
Students put letters in the correct order to form sight words.

Materials:
- pennies
- circle stickers
- index cards
- zipper bags

Activity Preparation

1. Determine a sight word for students to study.

2. Write the letters of the word on the circle stickers, one letter per sticker.

3. Place the stickers on the index card so they form the sight word.

4. Write the letters for the same word on a new set of stickers, one letter per sticker.

5. Place the second set of stickers on pennies, one sticker per penny.

6. Place the index card and the pennies in a zipper bag.

7. Follow this procedure to create as many card and penny sets as desired. Create a new zipper bag for each new sight word.

Activity Procedure

1. Give each student a zipper bag that contains pennies and an index card.

2. Instruct the student to remove the pennies and index card from the zipper bag and read the word on the index card.

3. Tell the student to turn the index card facedown on the table.

4. Have the student arrange the pennies to form the sight word. The student may self-check by looking at the index card. If the student is having trouble with the activity, allow him or her to look at the index card and make it a matching activity.

5. Students may exchange baggies and work on other words.

Adaptations

- Include the letters for a short sentence in each bag. Color-code each word so the students can easily sort the words.

- Place in a baggie five pennies that have uppercase letters on them, along with five matching lowercase letters. Have the students match uppercase letters to lowercase letters.

- Use the names of students instead of sight words. Place a photo of the child in the bag that contains the letters of his name.

Pin the Word on the Donkey

Skill:
Reading sight words

Suggested Group Size:
Whole class

Activity Overview:
Students tape tails that have sight words written on them onto a donkey.

Materials:
- "Donkey Poster and Tails" (pages 118–119)
- blindfold or scarf
- tape

Activity Preparation

1. Photocopy the "Donkey Poster" and color as desired (or print colored copies from the CD).

2. Cut out the pieces for the donkey poster and attach on the glue tab to make one large poster.

3. Photocopy as many copies of "Donkey Tails" as desired (or print colored copies from the CD).

4. Cut out the tails.

5. Determine sight words for students to study. Write the sight words on the donkey tails, one word per tail.

6. Laminate the poster and tails for durability.

Activity Procedure

1. Tape the donkey poster to a large whiteboard or chalkboard.

2. Have the students sit close to the board, but allow room for individual players.

3. Show a tail to the class and ask for a volunteer to read the word on it.

4. Have the student who read the word come up to the board.

5. Give him or her the tail with tape on the back of it.

6. Place a blindfold or scarf around his or her eyes. Spin him or her once and let him or her try to place the tail on the donkey. Once the tail has been placed, have the whole class read the word.

7. Have other students take turns following the same procedure. Once all the tails have been placed on the donkey, point to the words and read them together, one at a time.

Adaptations

- Have students clap out the number of syllables of each sight word.
- Create your own versions of the game by drawing a snowman or turkey on a poster board. Draw and cut out carrot noses or feathers with words written on them.
- Write letters or students' names on the tails.
- Write other concept words such as color words or number words on the tails.

Donkey Poster and Tails

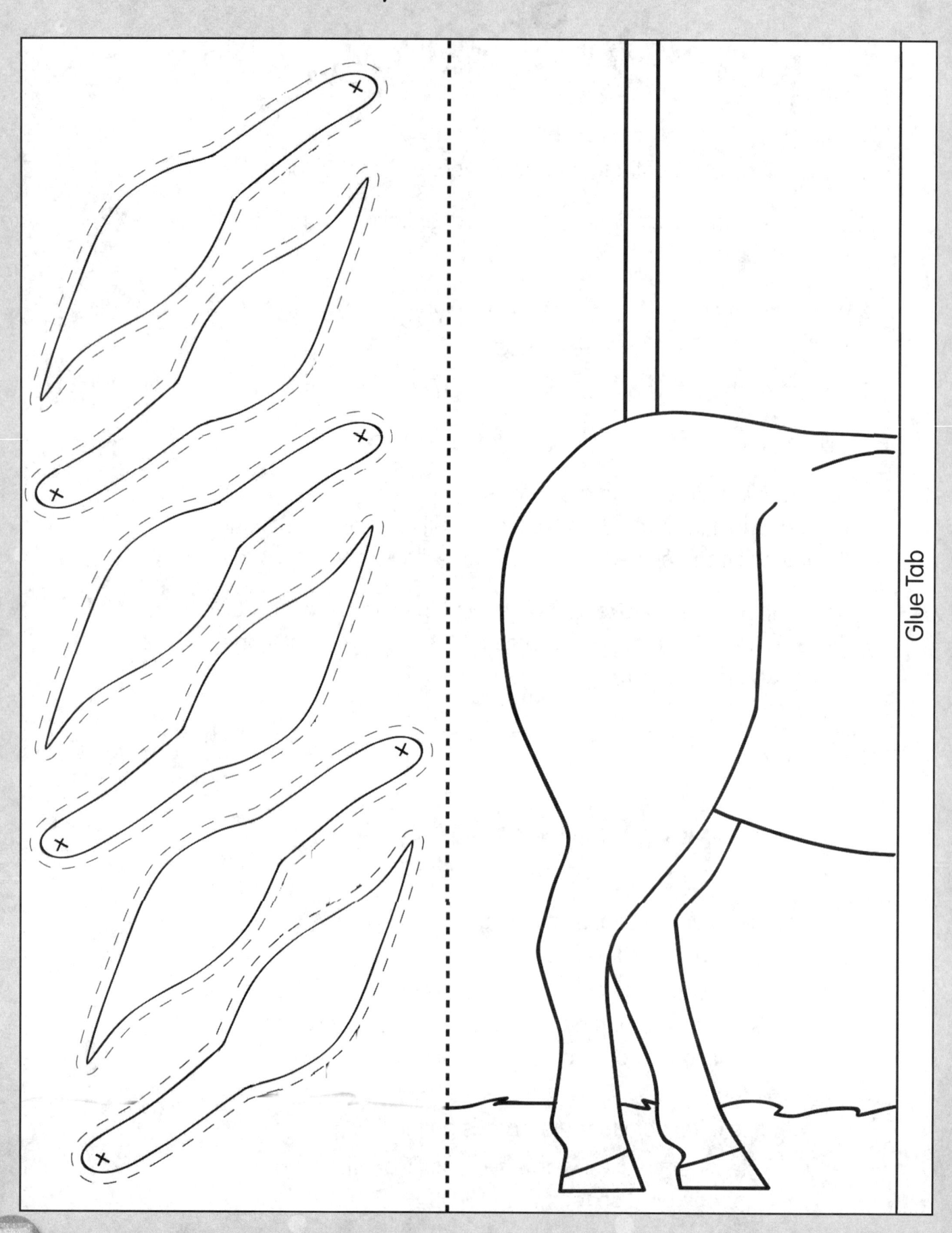

Glue Tab

Donkey Poster and Tails (cont.)

Go Fish

Skill:
Reading sight words

Suggested Group Size:
2–6 students

Activity Overview:
Students practice reading sight words as they gather two of the same word cards.

Materials:
- "Sight Word Cards" (pages 169–176)

Activity Preparation

1. Photocopy two sets of "Sight Word Cards" on cardstock paper.
2. Cut out the cards.
3. Laminate the cards for durability.

Activity Procedure

1. Shuffle the deck of cards and deal out two cards per student. Place the remaining cards in the center of the playing area.

2. Tell the students to look at their cards without showing them to others.

3. Have a student ask the other players for a word card that matches one of the word cards in his or her hand. If no one has that word, he or she needs to "Go Fish," which means to take the top card from the deck. If one of the players has the card, he or she must give it to the student who asked for it.

4. Once two matching cards have been gathered, they are placed on the table in a common area.

5. The student does not go again if he or she gets the requested card; instead, he or she waits for the next turn, once it comes around again. If at any time a student runs out of cards, he or she may take a card from the top of the deck. The game continues until all the cards have been placed into sets.

Adaptations

- Have a set consist of three cards instead of two cards.
- Have each student say a word that rhymes with the sight word as each set of cards is laid on the table.
- Use letter cards instead of word cards.
- Have the set consist of uppercase and lowercase letter cards.
- Have students match the uppercase letters to the lowercase letters.

Beat the Clock

Skill:
Forming sentences

Suggested Group Size:
2–4 students

Activity Overview:
Students are given one minute to form a sentence with word cards.

Materials:
- "Sight Word Cards" (pages 169–176)
- white index cards
- black marker
- 5 colored index cards
- clock or timer

Activity Preparation

1. Photocopy "Sight Word Cards" on cardstock paper.

2. Cut out the cards.

3. Write periods, question marks, and exclamation marks on the white index cards, writing one ending mark per card.

4. Laminate the cards for durability.

Activity Procedure

1. Spread out all the cards on a table. Be sure each word card is facing up.

2. Point to each word and have the students read it.

3. Tell the students that the blank cards are wild cards and that they can be any word.

4. Explain that the goal is to form at least one sentence in one minute. If time allows, another sentence can be formed.

5. Time students as they work together to form a sentence. Cards can be moved to a different part of the table when a sentence is formed.

6. Have the students read the sentence out loud when they are done.

Adaptations

- Lengthen or shorten time as needed.
- Use an egg timer (with sand) to give the students a designated three minutes.
- Include multiple cards of common sight words such as I, we, or like.
- Include other types of words, such as nouns and verbs—for example: friend, jump, skip.
- Have students work individually instead of in a group.

Question Game

Skill:
Forming sentences

Suggested Group Size:
2–4 students

Activity Overview:
Students arrange sight word cards in order to create a meaningful sentence.

Materials:
- "Question Game Sentences" (pages 126–129)
- zipper bags or envelopes

Activity Preparation

1. Photocopy each page of "Question Game Sentences" onto different-colored cardstock paper.

2. Cut out the word cards on each page.

3. Laminate for durability.

4. Place each set of like-colored words in its own zipper bag or envelope.

Activity Procedure

1. Give each student a zipper bag of colored words.

2. Tell the students they are to arrange the words in the zipper bag to form a sentence that makes a question.

3. Remind the students that a sentence starts with a capital letter and ends with an ending mark.

4. Guide students as necessary in forming sentences.

5. Have students read the sentences once they have been formed.

6. Exchange the zipper bags to allow students to form different sentences.

Adaptations

- Have students work in pairs.
- Write the words on colored tiles.
- Have students illustrate the sentences they form.
- Have students write an answer in response to the question.
- Have pairs of students combine the words in their baggies to come up with a new sentence.

Question Game Sentences

Did | the
little | boy
go | to
school | ?

Question Game Sentences (cont.)

What	would
you	like
to	do	?

Question Game Sentences (cont.)

Would you like to go play with them ?

Question Game Sentences (cont.)

How	do
you	get
to	her
house	?

Follow the Rainbow

Skill:
Forming sentences

Suggested Group Size:

2–7 students

Activity Overview:

Students practice reading sight words as they follow a rainbow.

Materials:

- "Follow the Rainbow," (pages 132–133)
- "Sight Word Cards" (pages 169–176)
- pot
- buttons or other space markers

Activity Preparation

1. Photocopy "Follow the Rainbow" on cardstock paper and color as desired (or print colored copies from the CD).

2. Attach the two game board pages together on the glue tab to form one large game board.

3. Photocopy "Sight Word Cards" on cardstock paper.

4. Cut out the word cards

5. Laminate the game boards and word cards for durability.

6. Place the cards in the pot.

Activity Procedure

1. Place the "Follow the Rainbow" game board in a central location.

2. Place the pot in a central location.

3. Provide each student with a space marker to place at the beginning of the rainbow.

4. Have a student select a sight word card from the pot. If he or she can read the word, he or she may move his or her space marker one space along the rainbow and keep the card. If he or she cannot read the card, have him or her return the card to the pot.

5. Have other students take turns following the same procedure.

6. Continue until all the students have reached the end of the rainbow.

7. Have students look at the words they collected to try to form a sentence.

8. Have students read their sentences out loud.

Adaptations

- Provide each student with a blank card that can be used as a wild card when forming sentences.
- Have students identify the vowels in each sight word.
- Use letter cards instead of words.
- If using letters, have students put the letters in alphabetical order at the end of the activity.

Follow the Rainbow

Follow the

Glue Tab

#50698 Early Childhood Reading Activities © Shell Education

Follow the Rainbow (cont.)

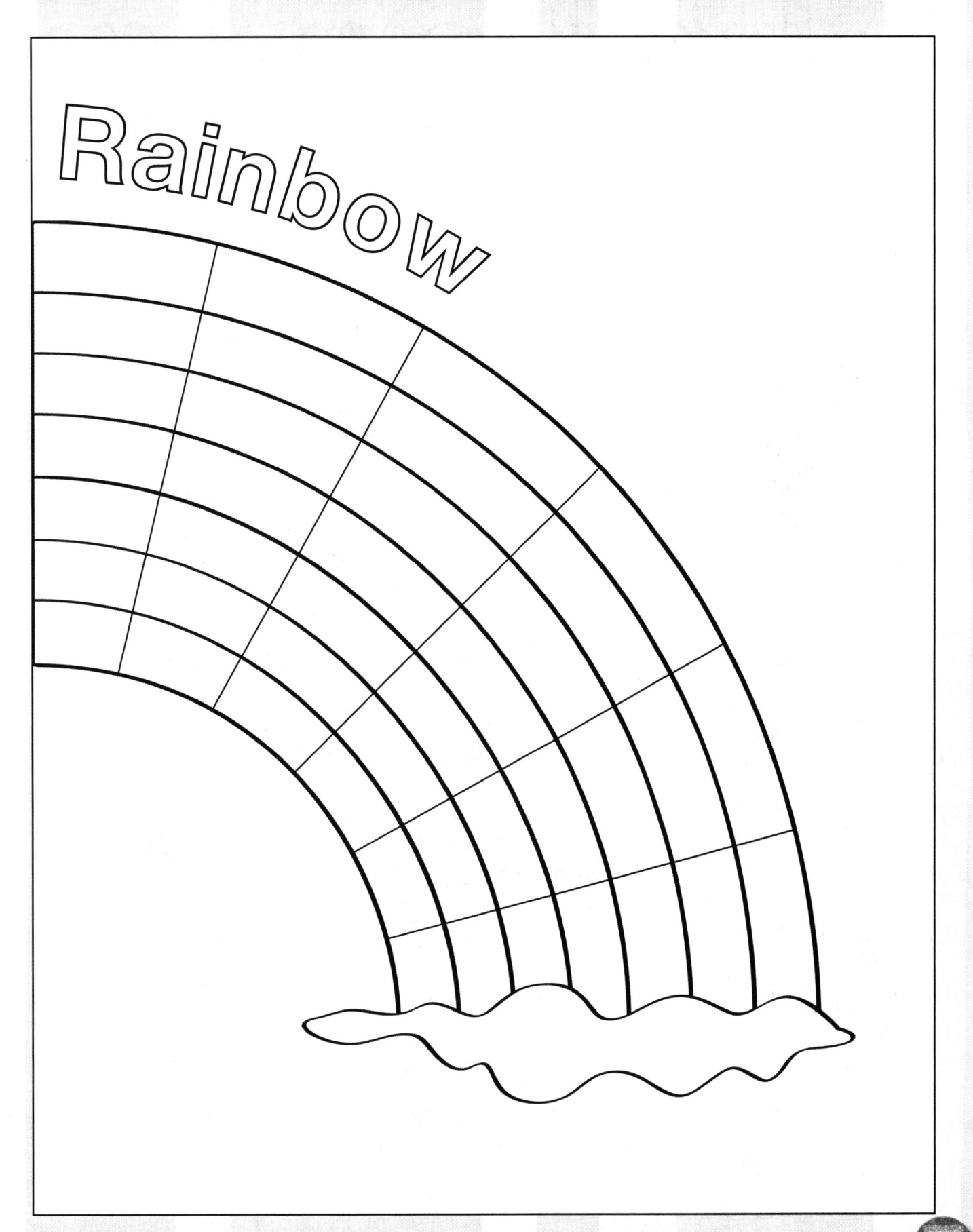

Rainbow

It's Raining

Skill:
Forming Sentences

Suggested Group Size:

2–4 students

Activity Overview:

Students match sight words on raindrops to sight words in a sentence on a puddle.

Materials:

- "It's Raining" Game Mats (pages 136–139)
- "Raindrops" (pages 140–141)

Activity Preparation

1. Photocopy "It's Raining" and "Raindrops" on cardstock paper and color as desired (or print colored copies from the CD).

2. Cut out the raindrops.

3. Laminate the game mats and raindrop cards for durability.

Activity Procedure

1. Provide each student with a game mat.

2. Place all the raindrops facedown in a central location.

3. Have a student select a raindrop from the raindrop collection. If the student can read the word, he or she may keep it. If the word on the raindrop matches a word in the student's sentence, he or she may place it in the puddle. If the word does not match a word in the sentence, he or she may place the raindrop on his or her cloud. If the student cannot read the word, he or she returns the raindrop to the pile.

4. Have other students take turns and follow the same procedure. If a student sees a word on another player's cloud that is in his or her sentence, the student may take that word when it is his or her turn.

5. Play continues until all the raindrops have been placed with their matching sentences.

Adaptations

- Have students clap out the number of syllables in each sight word.
- Create durable raindrops out of foam.
- When a raindrop is selected that does not match a word on the puddle, instead of placing it on the cloud, put it back into the raindrop collection.
- Have students illustrate the sentences.

It's Raining — Game Mat 1

We went with him.

It's Raining — Game Mat 2

It was for her.

It's Raining Game — Mat 3

They play with me.

It's Raining Game — Mat 4

Is this for you?

Raindrops

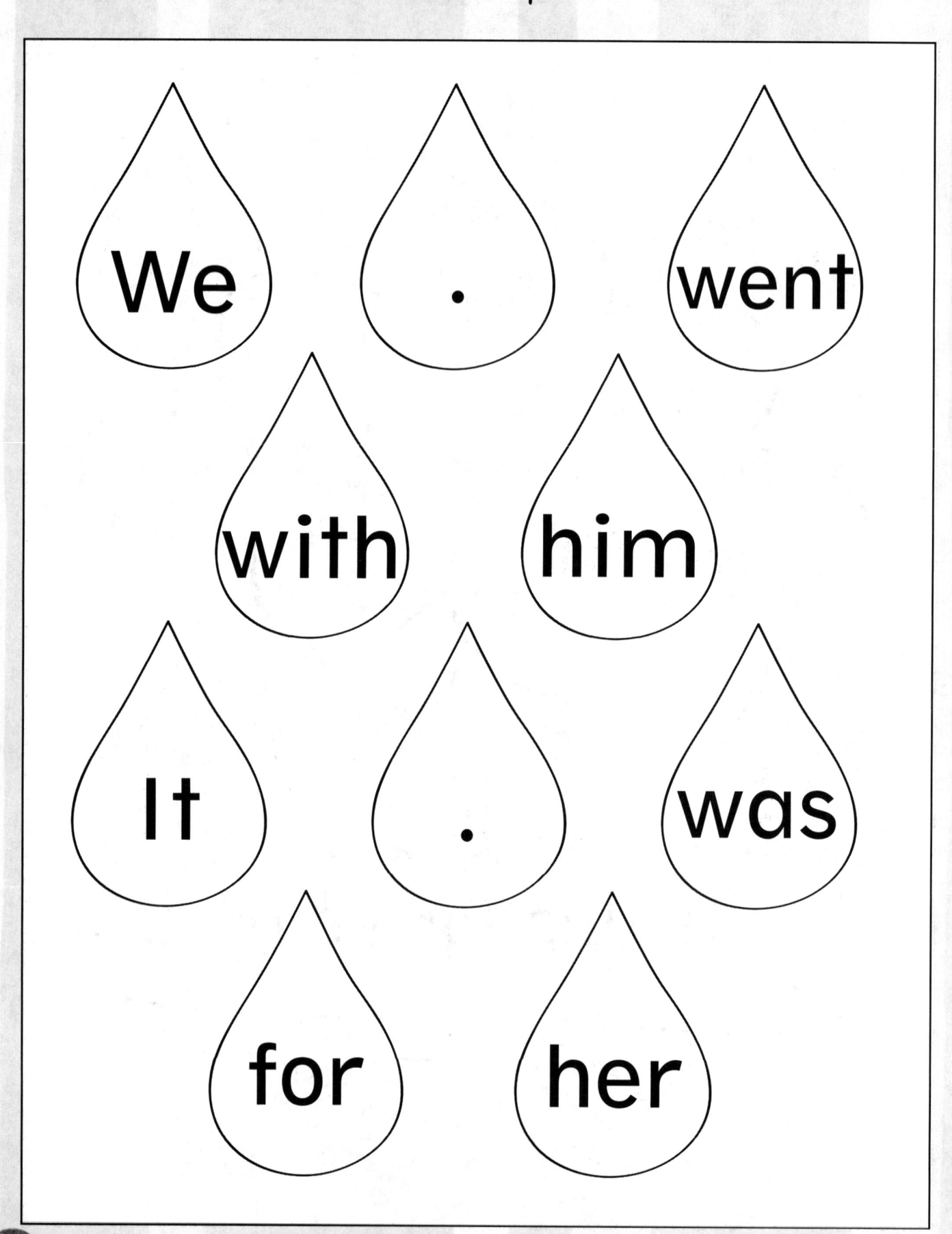

We . went

with him

It . was

for her

Raindrops (cont.)

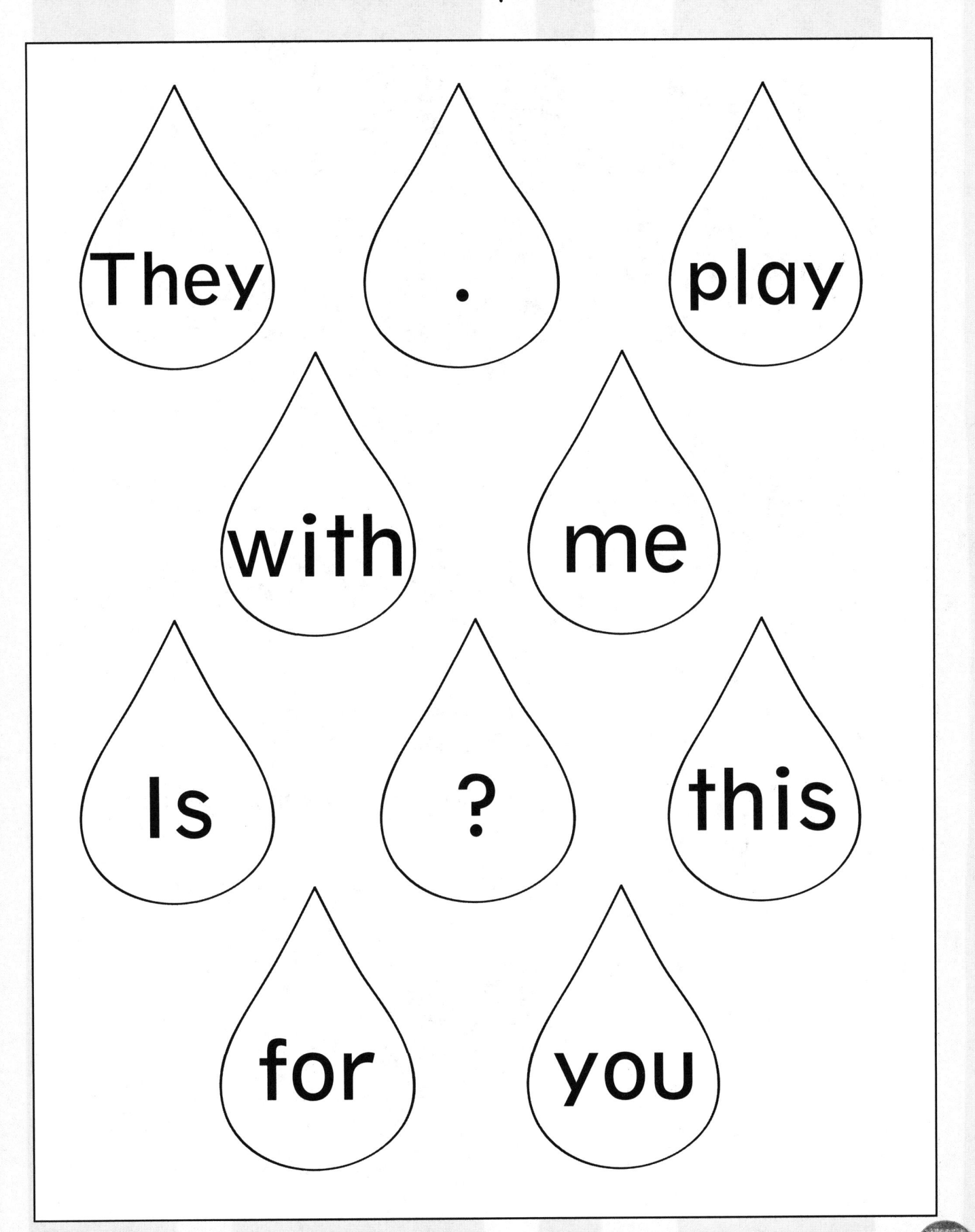

- They
- .
- play
- with
- me
- Is
- ?
- this
- for
- you

Puzzle Words

Skill:
Forming sentences

Suggested Group Size:
2–3 students

Activity Overview:
Students put puzzle pieces together by reading sight words that form a sentence.

Materials:
- "Puzzle Patterns" (pages 144–146)
- zipper bags

Activity Preparation

1. Photocopy each page of "Puzzle Patterns" on different colored cardstock paper.

2. Cut out the puzzle pieces and laminate for durability.

3. Place individual puzzles into zipper bags.

Activity Procedure

1. Provide each student with a zipper bag containing a puzzle.

2. Tell the students to put their puzzles together. Assist as needed.

3. Have the students read their puzzles once they have put them together.

4. Exchange puzzles.

Adaptations

- Use the blank puzzle (page 147) to create your own sentences.
- Have the students write a word on a piece of paper and then draw lines to create their own puzzles. Then they may cut it out and put it back together again.
- Have students glue the puzzle pieces on a piece of paper.
- Purchase premade cardboard puzzles from a craft store and create your own sentences.

Puzzle Pattern — 1

We can help her.

Puzzle Pattern — 2

Where **did**

she **go?**

Puzzle Pattern — 3

We want to go out to play.

Blank Puzzle Pattern

Word Roundup

Skill:
Forming sentences

Suggested Group Size:
2–5 students

Activity Overview:
Students select word cards and match them to words on a game mat.

Materials:
- "Word Roundup" Game Mat (pages 150–151)
- "Word Roundup" Cards (pages 152–153)

Activity Preparation

1. Photocopy "Word Roundup" and "Word Roundup Cards" onto cardstock paper.

2. Cut out game mats and word cards.

3. Glue the two pieces of the game mat together on the glue tab to create one large game mat.

4. Laminate the game mat and cards for durability.

Activity Procedure

1. Place the game mat in central location. Place the word cards face down near the game mat.

2. Point to the words in the sentences as you and the students read them.

3. Have a student select a word card from the stack and read the word. If the student can read the word, he or she should place it on top of the matching word on the game mat. If the student cannot read the word, read it together as a group. Place the word card at the bottom of the stack of cards.

4. Have other students take turns following the same procedure.

5. Once all of the cards have been matched, read the sentences again as a group.

Adaptations

- Use colored cardstock paper for the word cards, using a different color for each sentence.
- Create your own game mat and letters using the names of students in the class.
- Have students write and illustrate one of the completed sentences on paper.

Word Roundup Game Mat

We like to play.

I see my cat.

I have a big dog.

Glue Tab

Word Roundup Game Mat (cont.)

| School is fun. | My house is green. | I want to go home. |

Word Roundup Word Cards

We	like	to
play.	I	see	my
cat.	I	have
a	big	dog.

Word Roundup Word Cards (cont.)

School	is	fun
My	house	is
green.	I	want
to	go	home.

References Cited

Buehler, Ruth M.C. 1992. Making school fun for you and your students. ERIC Document ED349302.

Burns, Susan M., Peg Griffin, and Catherine E. Snow. 1998. Preventing reading difficulties in young children. National Research Council. Washington D.C.: National Academy Press.

———1999. Starting out right: A guide to promoting children's reading success Washington DC: National Academy Press.

Carter, Susanne. 2002. The impact of parent/family involvement of student outcomes: An annotated bibliography of research from the past decade. Eugene, OR: Consortium for Appropriate Dispute Resolution in Special Education. ERIC Document 476296.

Dakin, Alexandra B. 1999. The effectiveness of a skill based explicit phonics reading program K-2 as measured by student performance and teacher evaluation. Master's thesis, Dominican College. ERIC Document ED430215.

Dwyer, Edward J., and Elizabeth Ralston. 1999. Teaching students to use phonics effectively with emphasis on rimes and onsets. ERIC Document ED 435091.

Ehri, Linnea C. 2005. Learning to read words: Theory, findings, and issues. Mahwah, NJ: Lawrence Eribaum Associates, Inc.

Monroe, Johnna, and Jeannine Staunton. 2000. Improving student reading skills through sight word instruction. M. A. Research Project, Saint Xavier University and Skylight Professional Development. ERIC Document ED443101.

Robinson, Susan S. 1991. Reading achievement: Contributions of invented spelling and alphabetic knowledge. ERIC Document ED331021.

Shaver, Ann V., and Richard T. Walls. 1998. Effect of Title I parent involvement on student reading and mathematics achievement. *Journal of Research and Development in Education.* ERIC Document EJ561992.

Wylie, Richard E. 1969. Associated factors of word element perception as they relate to success in beginning reading. ERIC Document ED033004.

Yopp, Hallie K., and Ruth K. Yopp. 2000. Supporting phonemic awareness development in the classroom. *The Reading Teacher* 54 (2): 130–143.

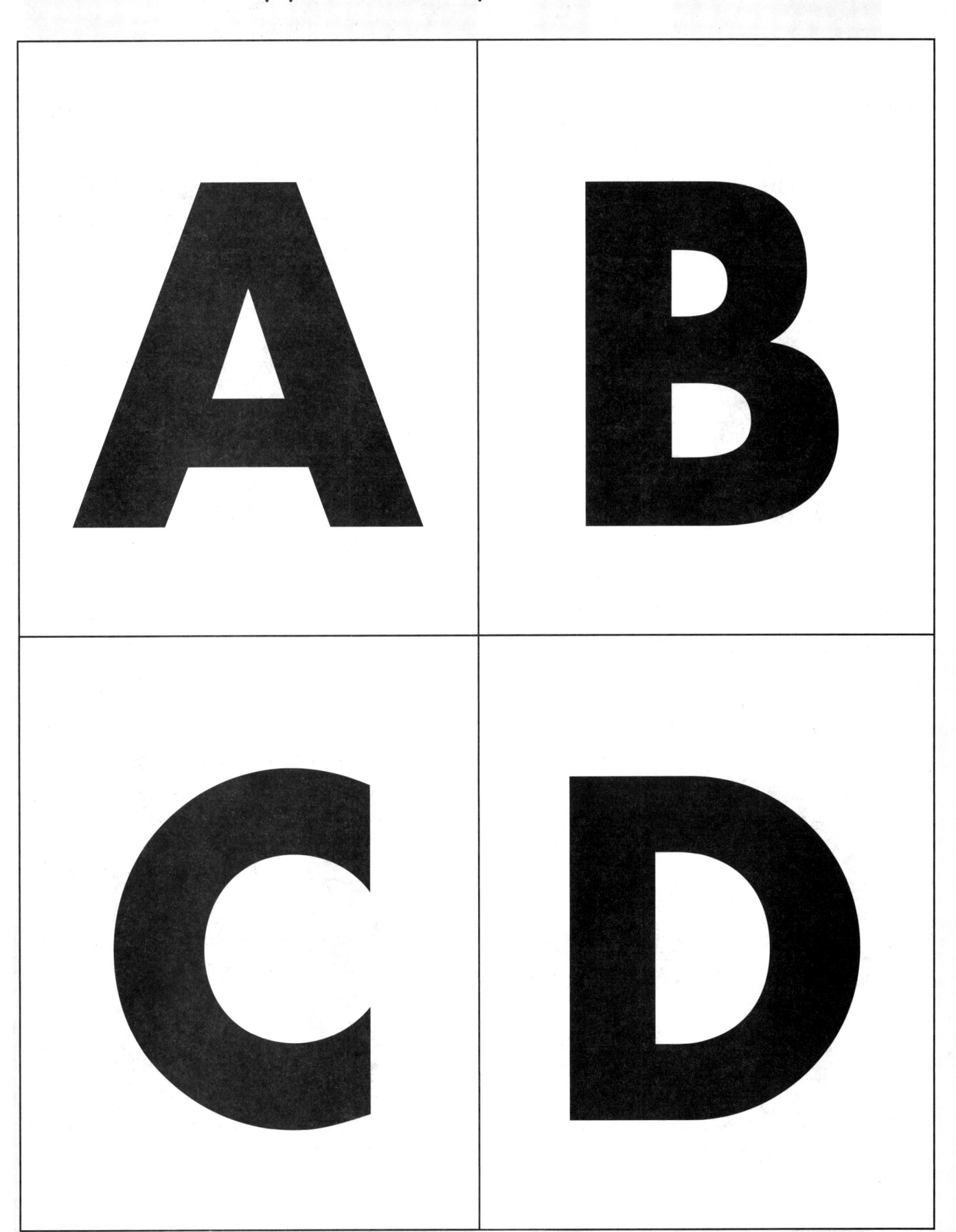

Uppercase Alphabet Cards

| A | B |
| C | D |

© Shell Education   #50698 Early Childhood Reading Activities

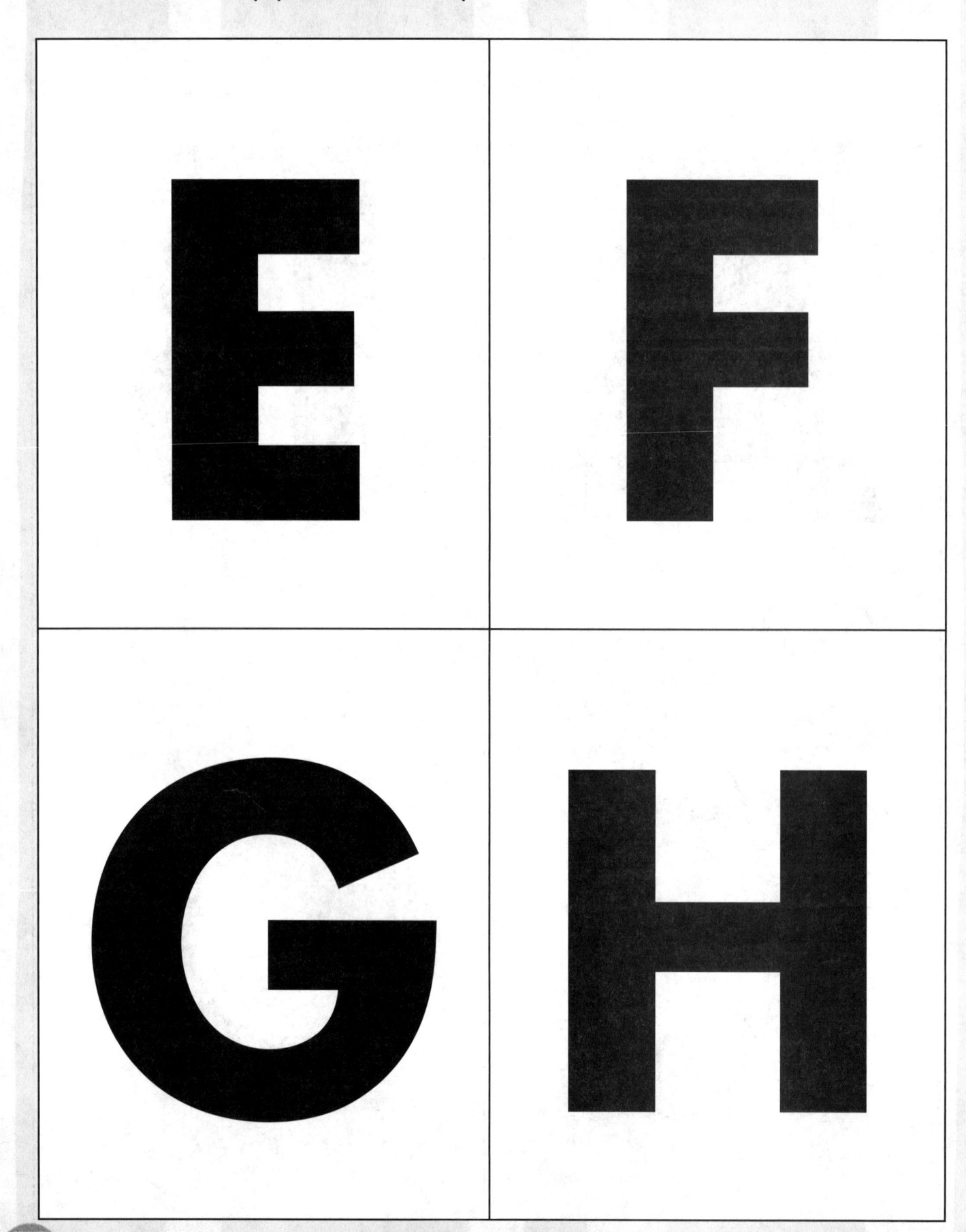

Uppercase Alphabet Cards (cont.)

E	F
G	H

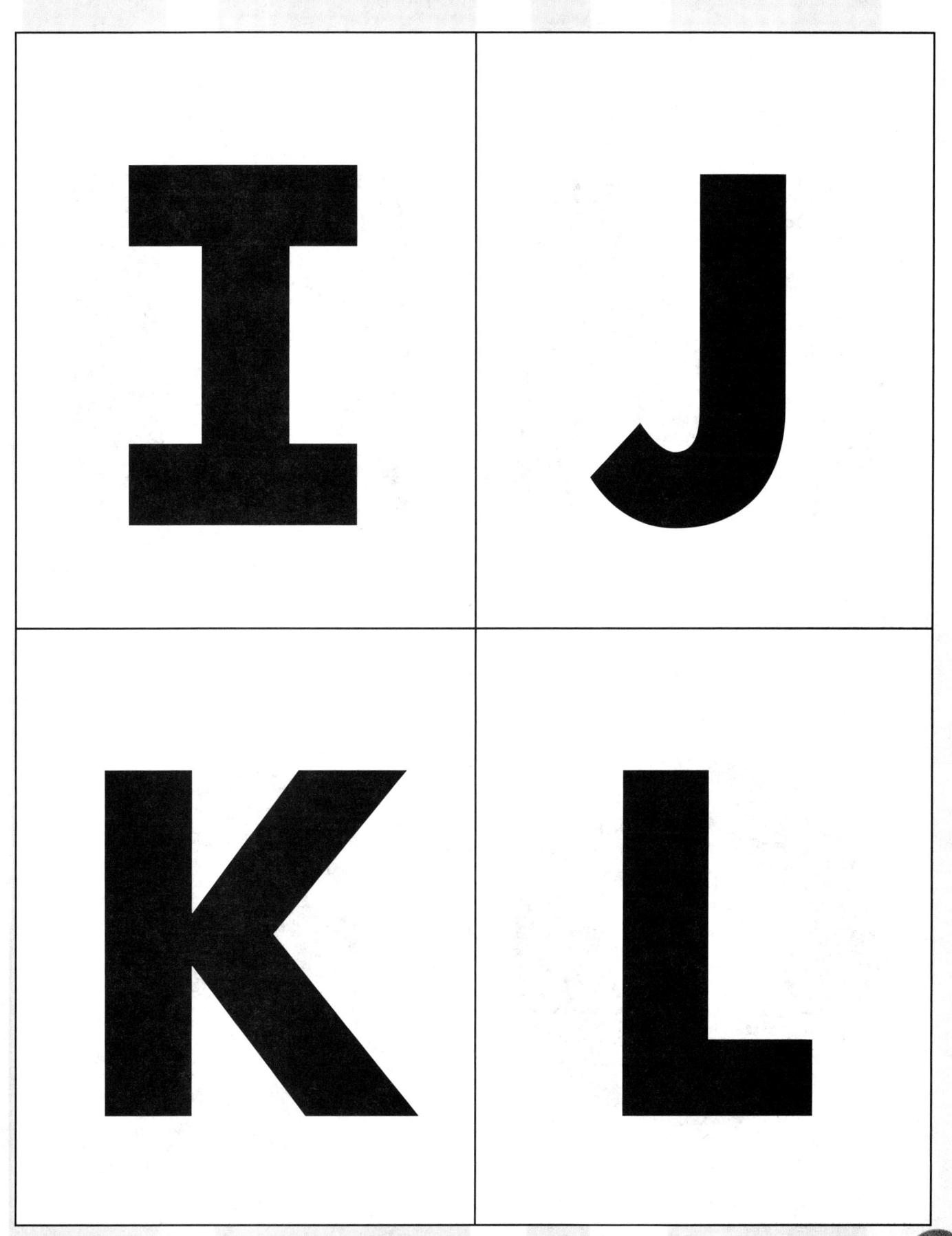

Uppercase Alphabet Cards (cont.)

I

J

K

L

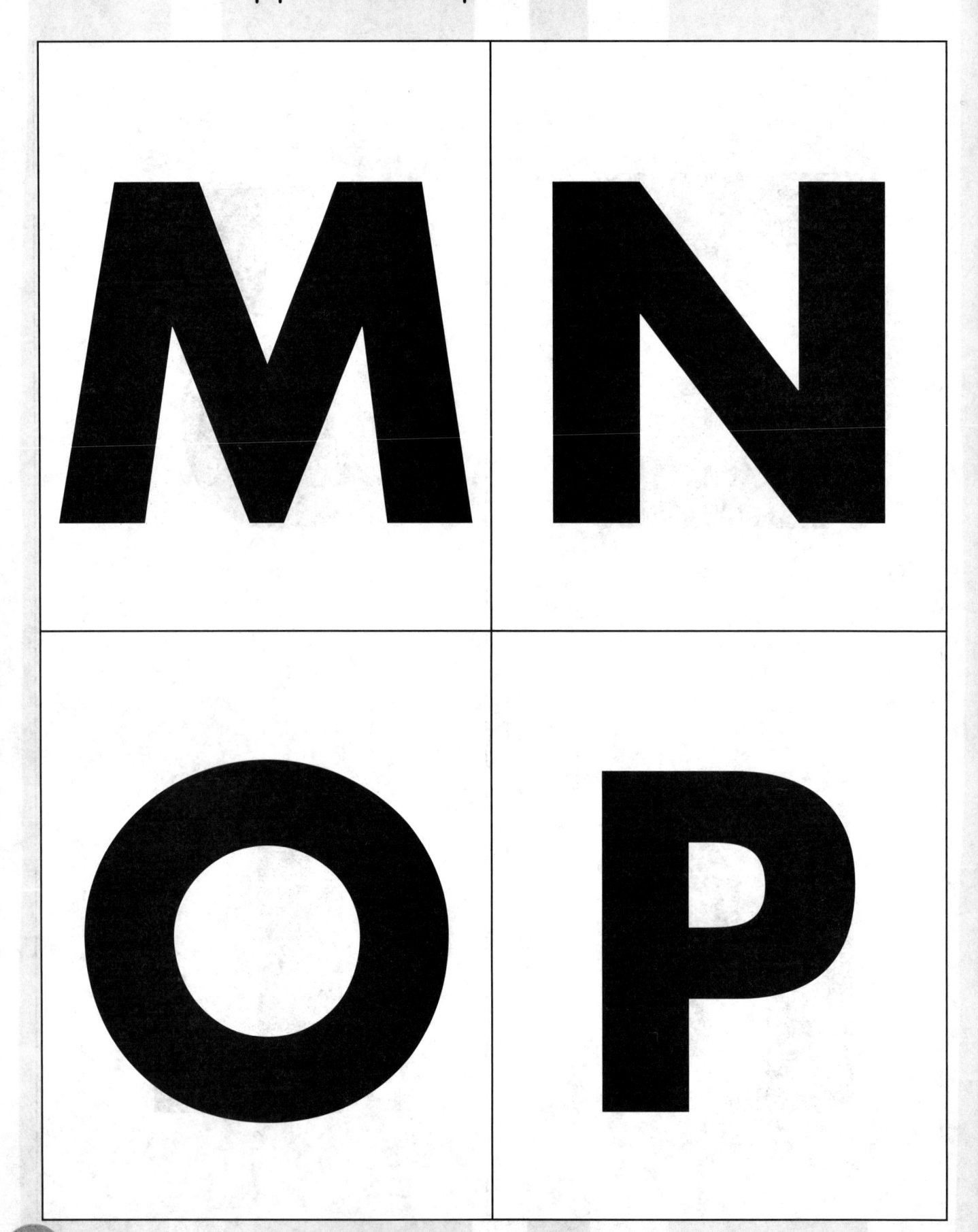

Uppercase Alphabet Cards (cont.)

M   N

O   P

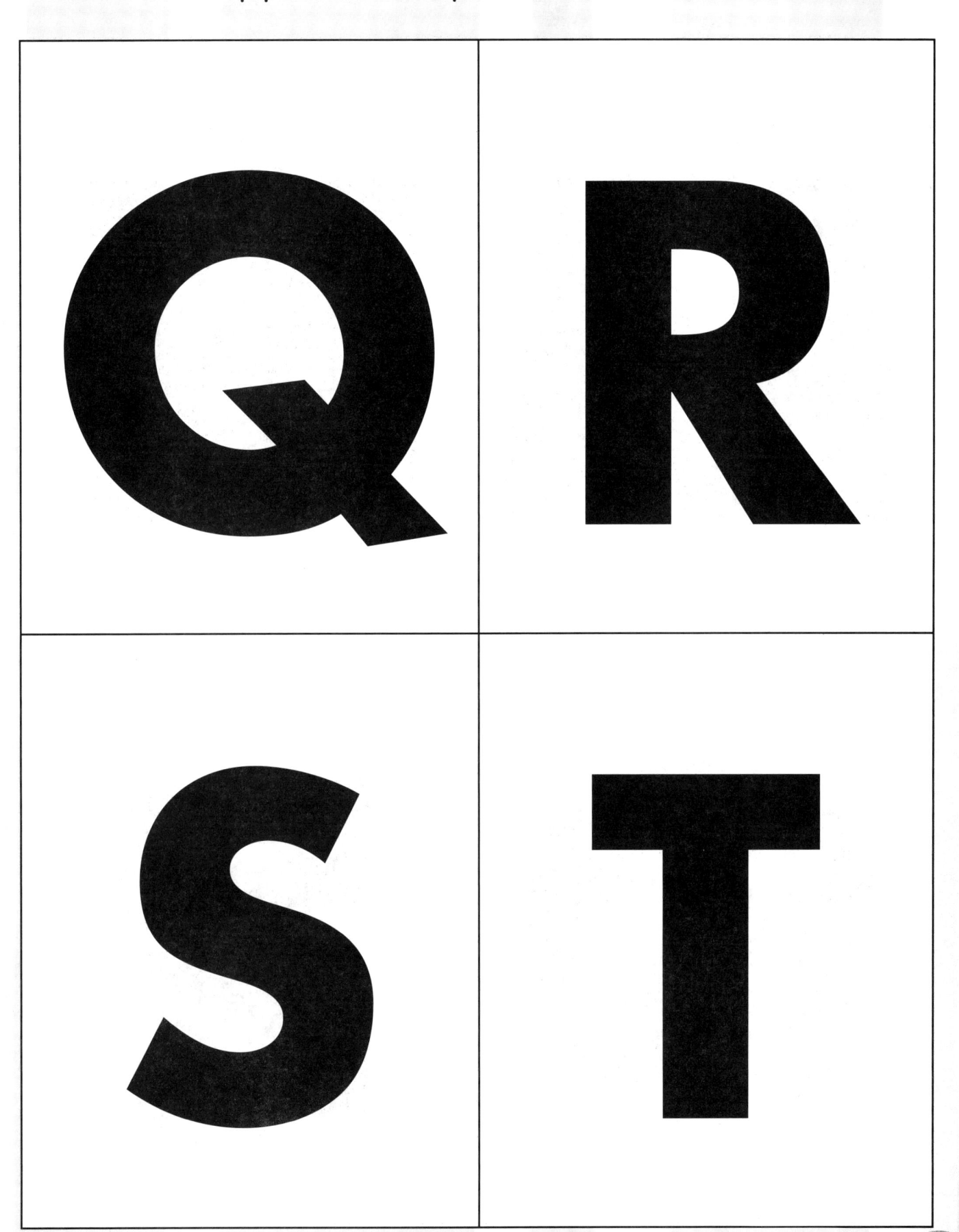

Uppercase Alphabet Cards (cont.)

Q R

S T

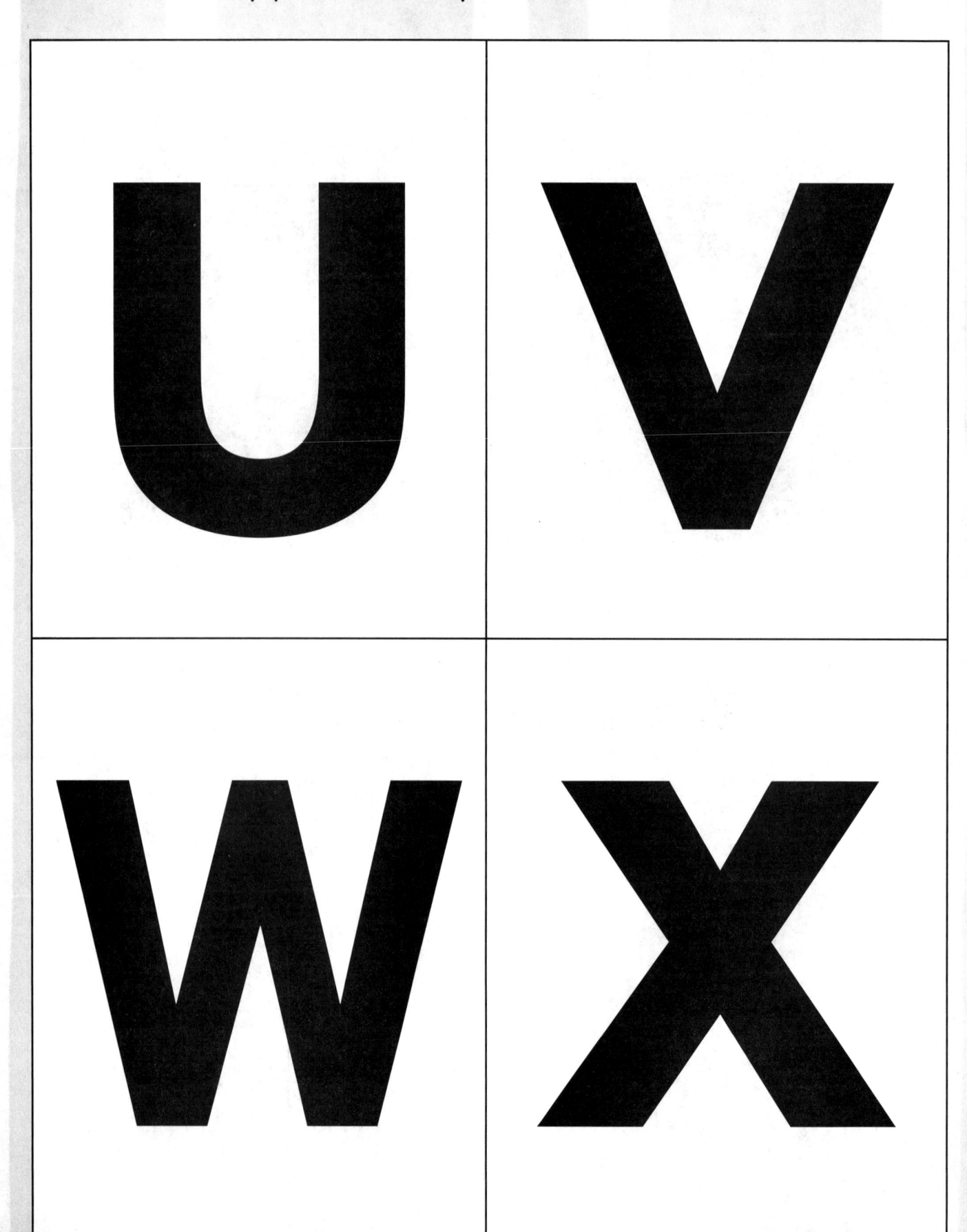

Uppercase Alphabet Cards (cont.)

U V

W X

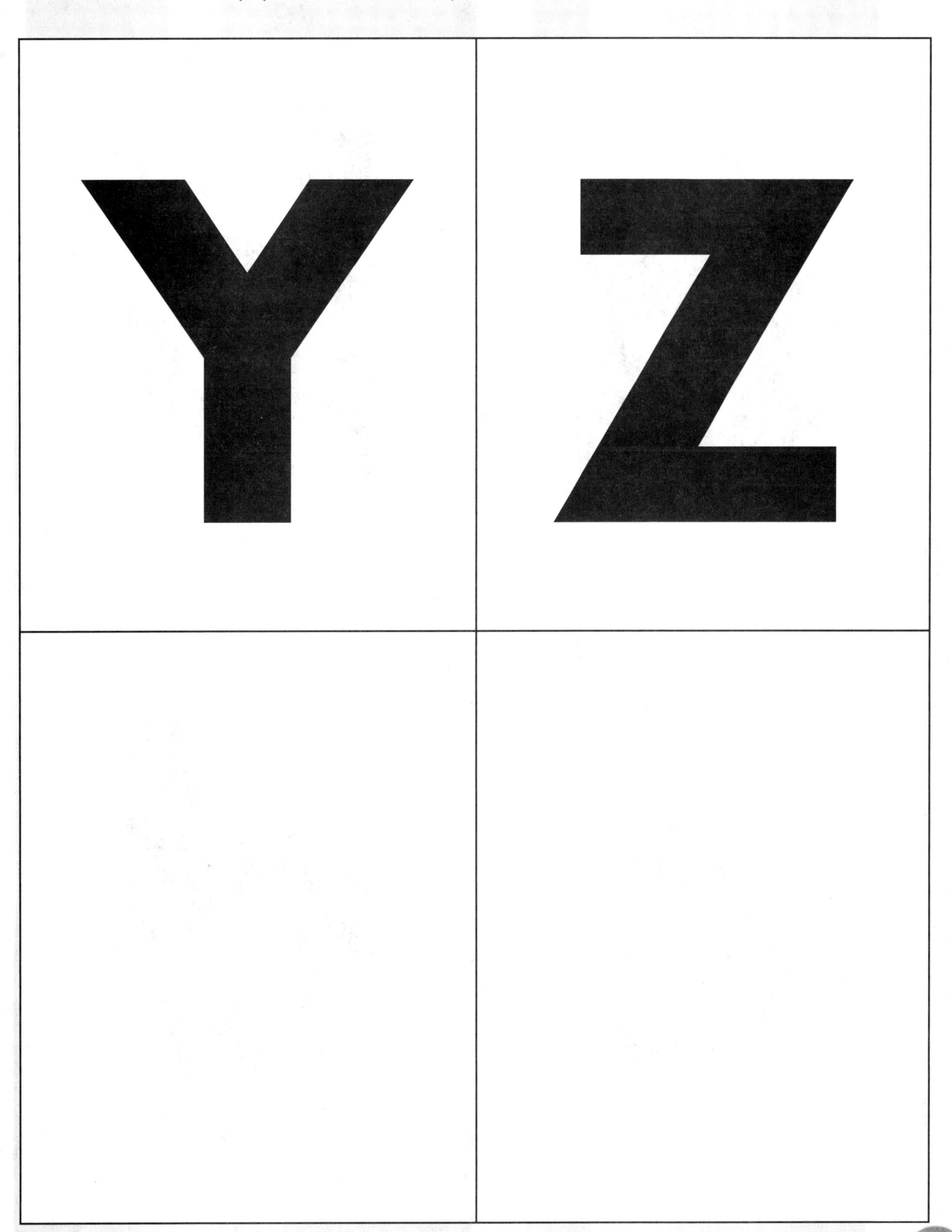

Uppercase Alphabet Cards (cont.)

Y   Z

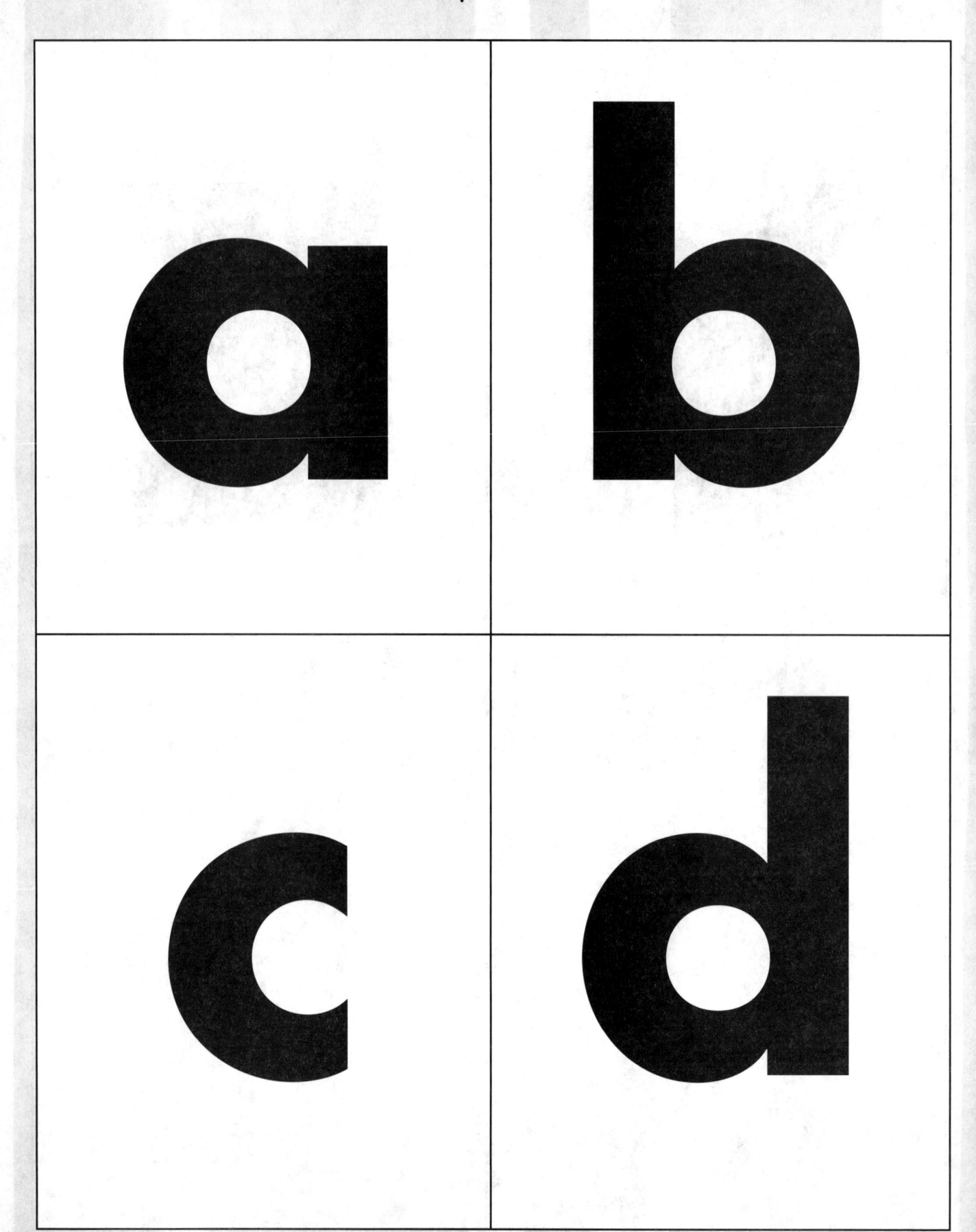

Lowercase Alphabet Cards (cont.)

a	b
c	d

Lowercase Alphabet Cards (cont.)

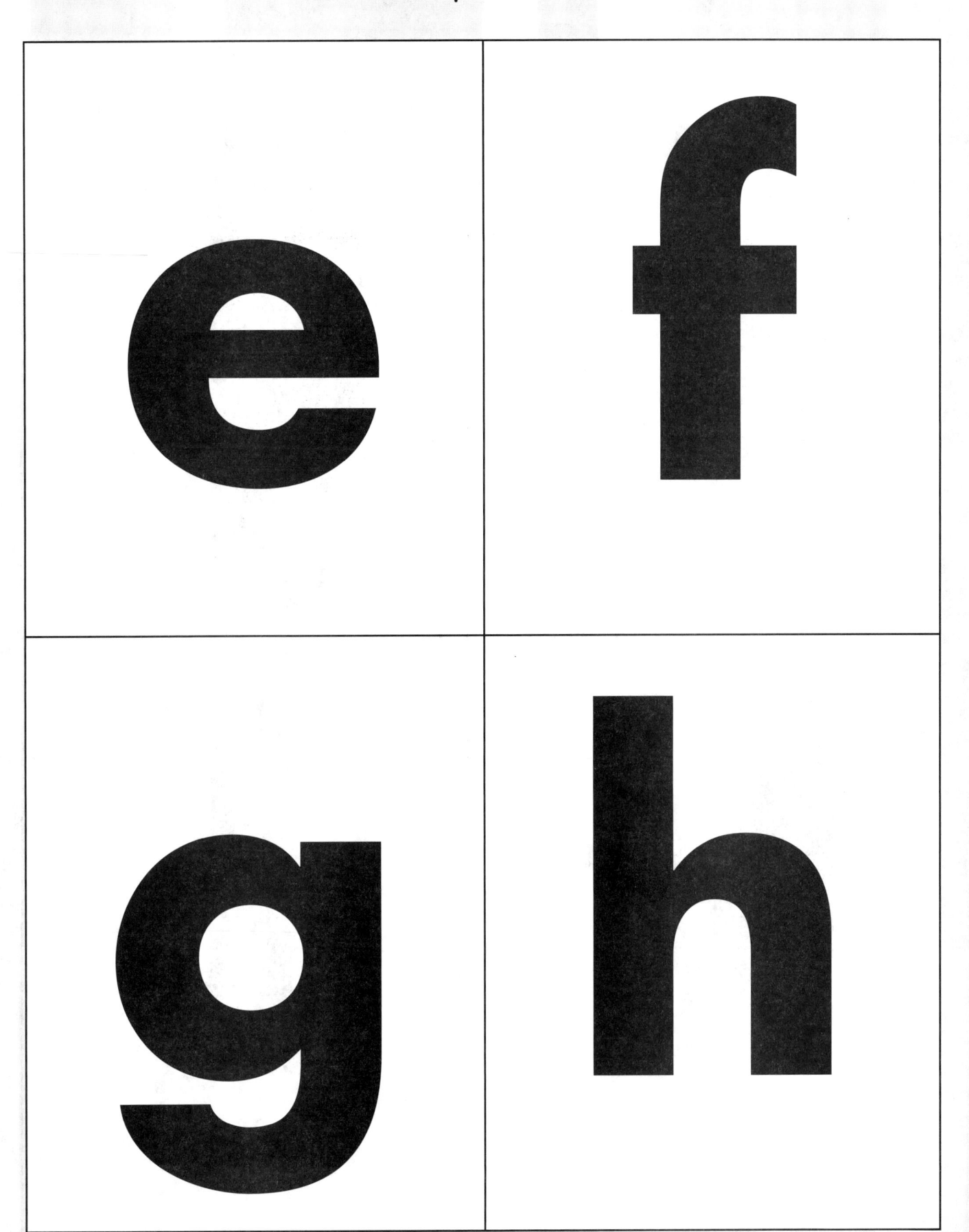

Lowercase Alphabet Cards (cont.)

e	f
g	h

© Shell Education #50698 Early Childhood Reading Activities

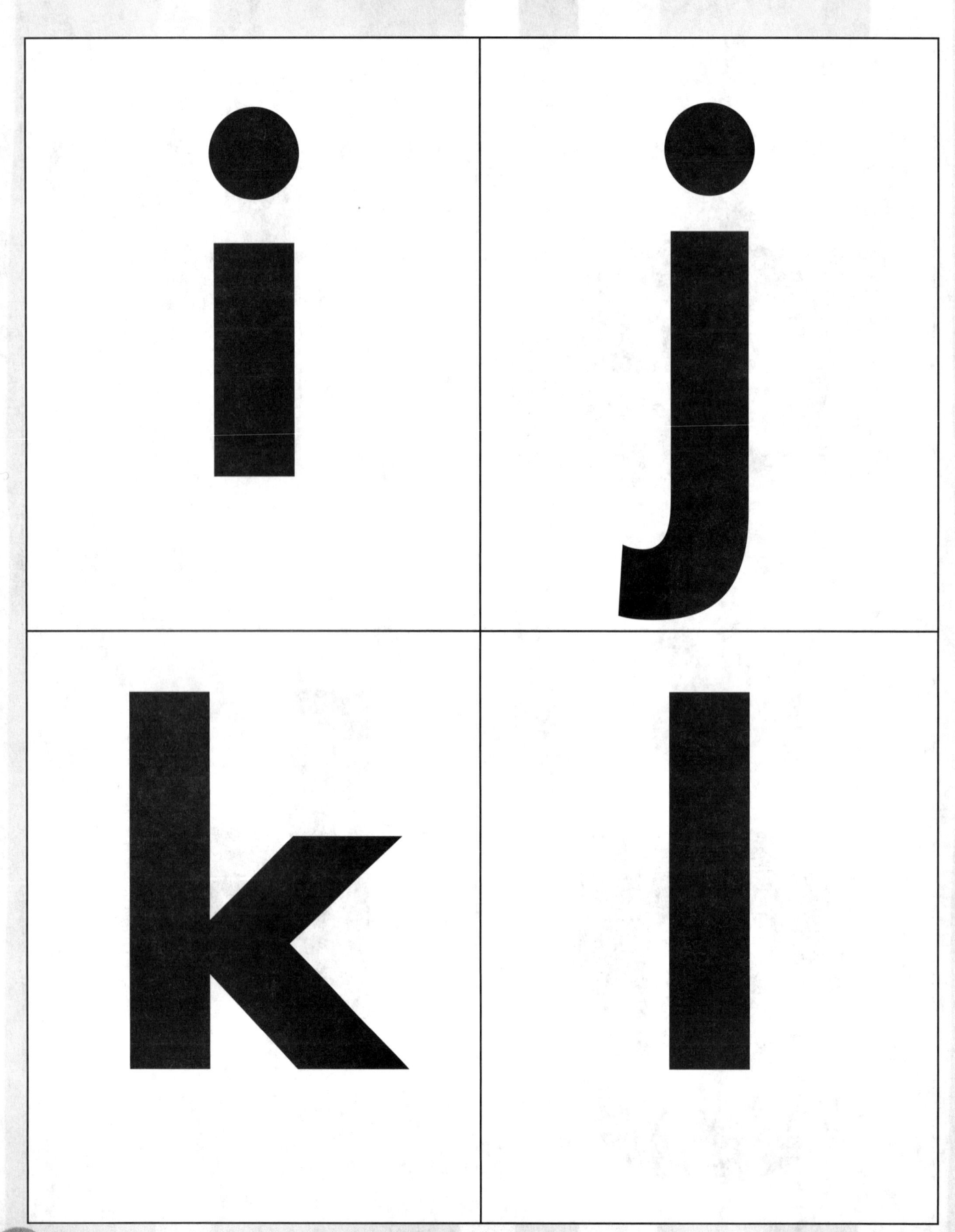

Lowercase Alphabet Cards (cont.)

i	j
k	l

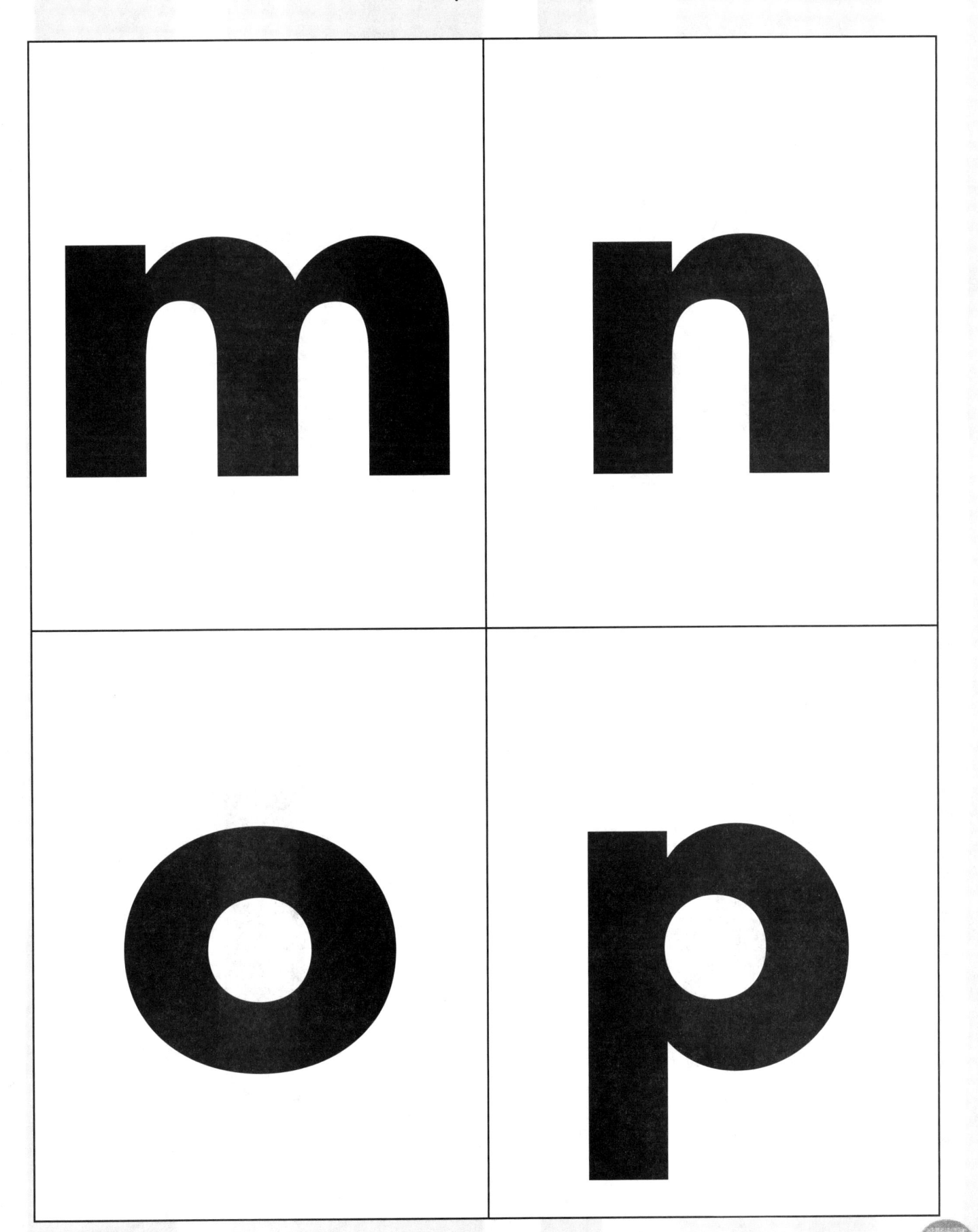

Lowercase Alphabet Cards (cont.)

m	n
o	p

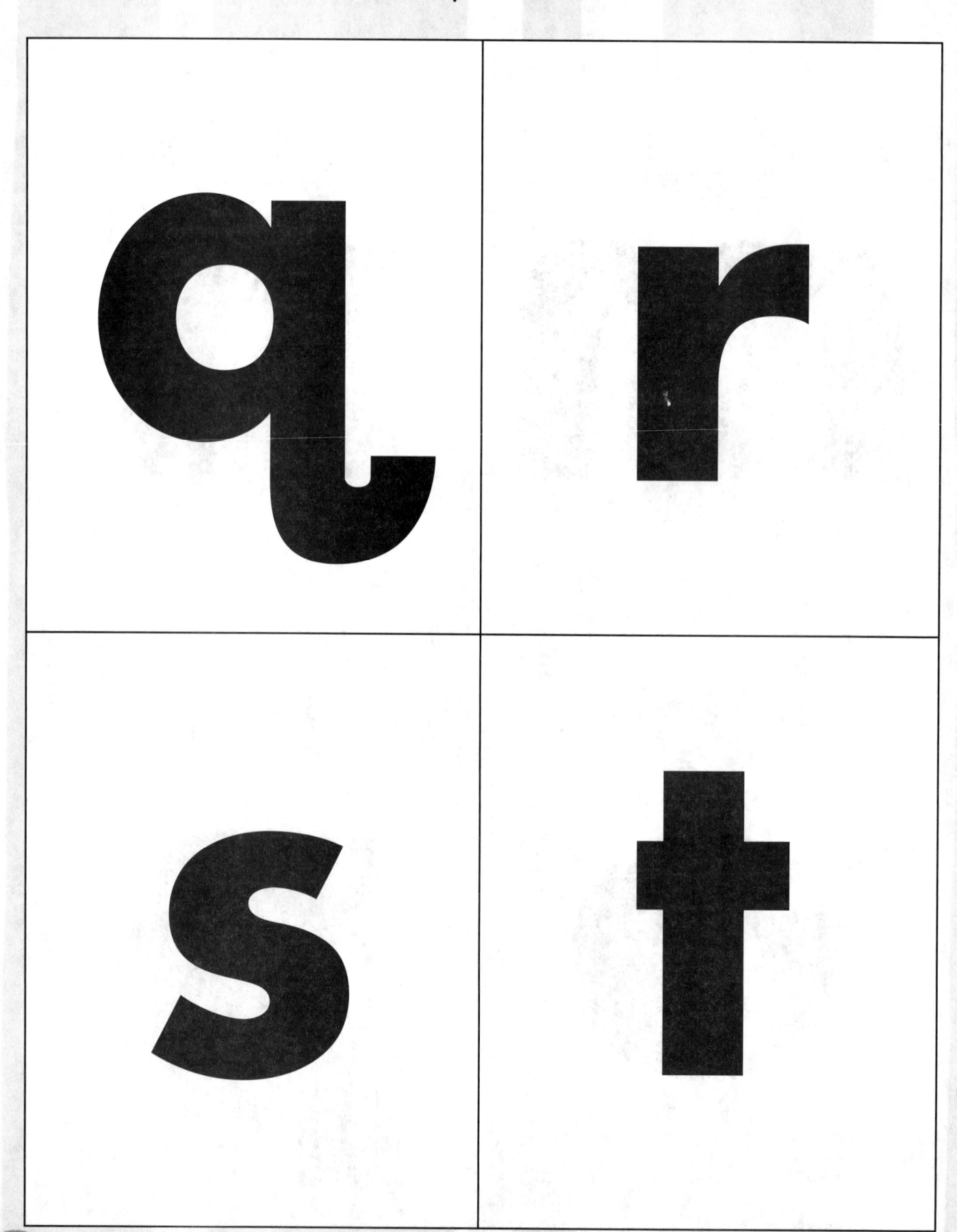

Lowercase Alphabet Cards (cont.)

| q | r |
| s | t |

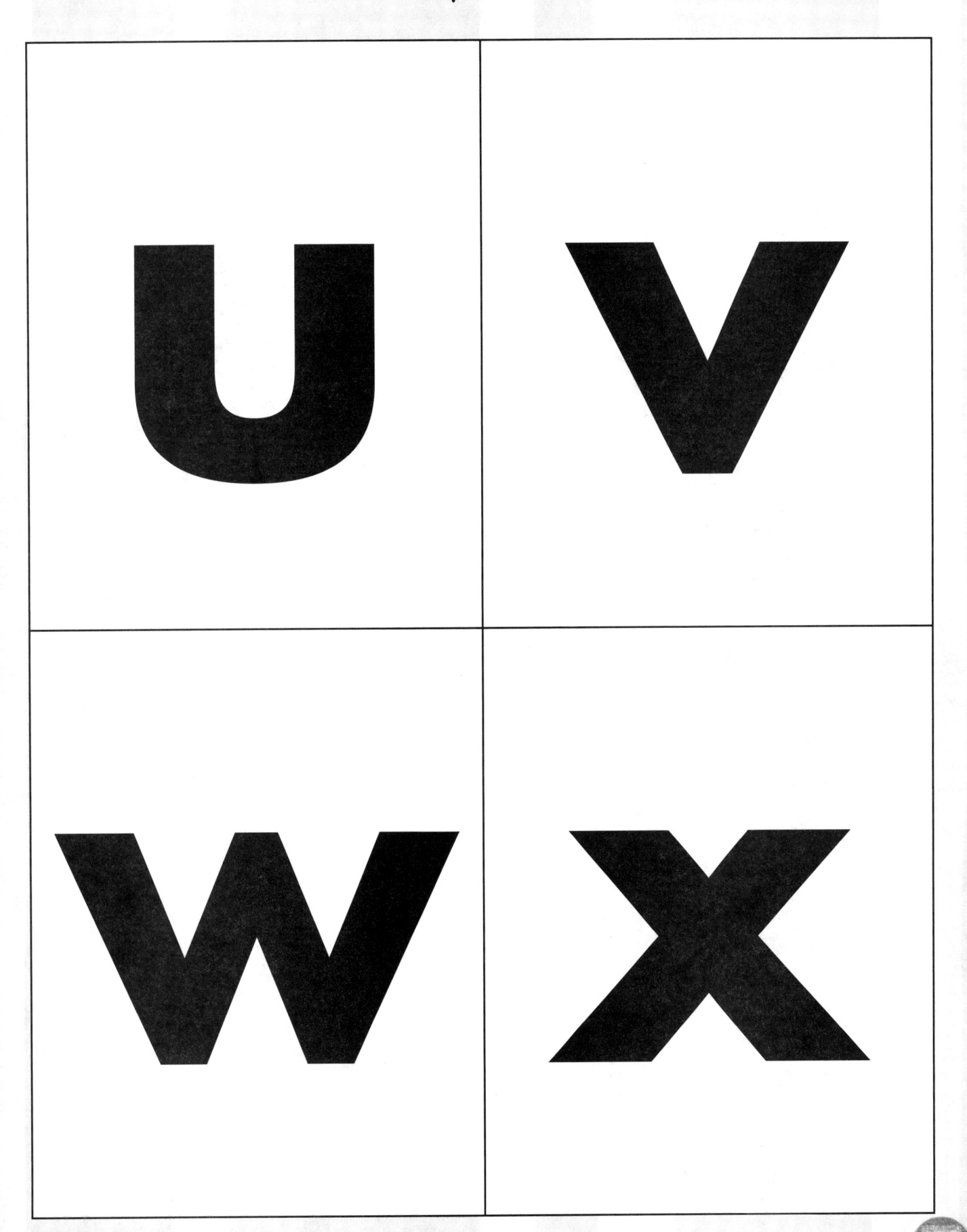

Lowercase Alphabet Cards (cont.)

u   v

w   x

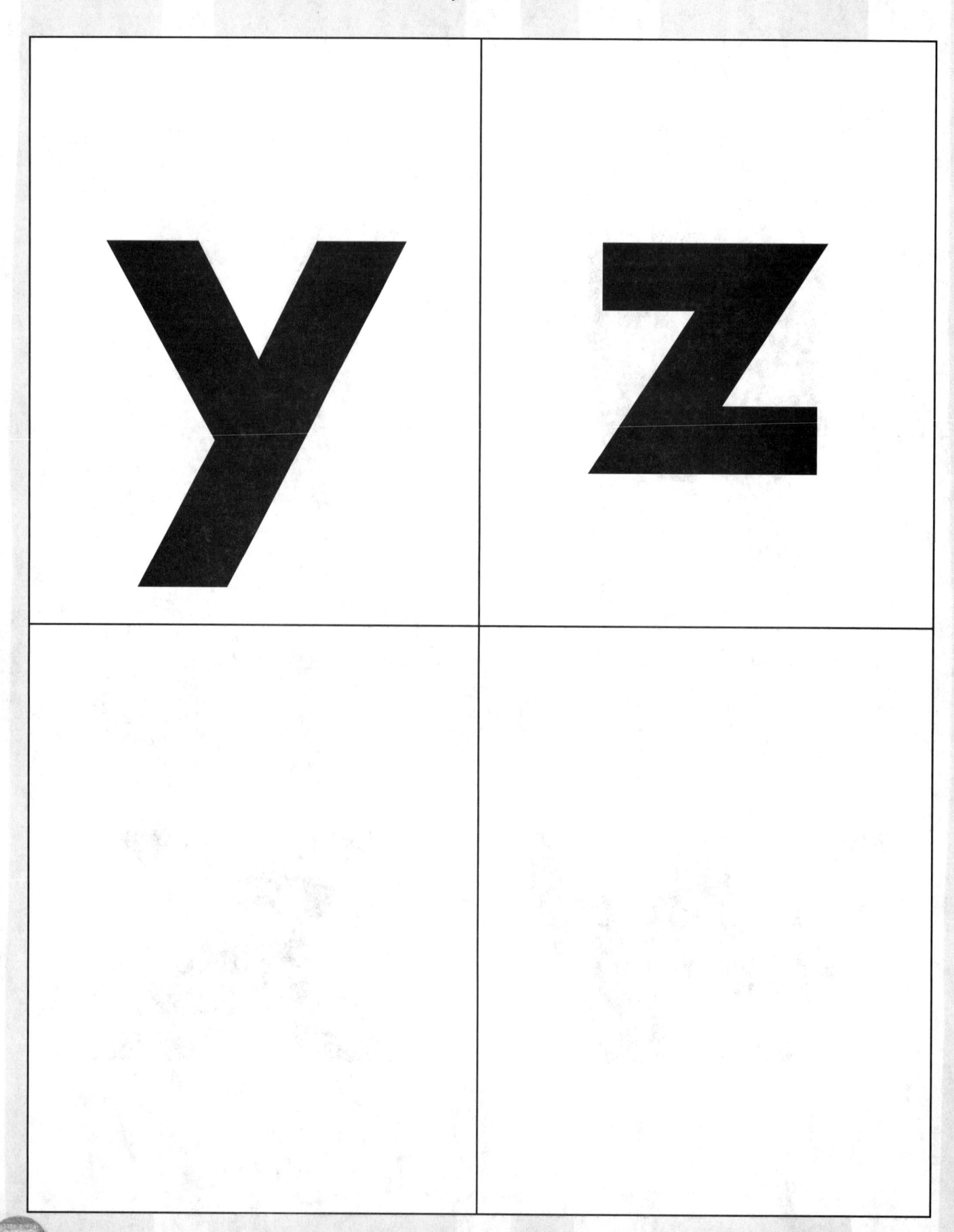

Lowercase Alphabet Cards (cont.)

y | z

Lowercase Alphabet Cards (cont.)

Sight Word Cards

a	all
an	and
are	as

Sight Word Cards (cont.)

at	be
but	by
can	each

Sight Word Cards (cont.)

for	had
have	he
his	how

Sight Word Cards (cont.)

I	in
is	it
of	on

Sight Word Cards (cont.)

one	or
other	out
said	she

Sight Word Cards (cont.)

some	that
the	there
they	this

Sight Word Cards (cont.)

to	**use**
up	**was**
we	**went**

Sight Word Cards (cont.)

were	what
when	with
you	yours